JonBenét

The final chapter

JonBenét

JonBenét

Marcel Elfers
Master Profiler through written communication

JonBenét

1st update (January 2021):
- Poem added.
- Minor spelling errors correction.
- Sentence construction improvements.
- Increased contrast in the graphics.

2nd update (February 2021):
- Minor sentence construction improvements
- Laurence Smith plea bargain claim added

Printed by CreateSpace, an Amazon.com Company
Available on Amazon.com

For Pepper

Every abused child deserves justice

About the Author

Marcel Elfers was born in Haarlem, the Netherlands, and moved to the United States in the mid-eighties as a Physical Therapist.
He has always been intrigued by what motivates people into action with a focus on criminals. He wrote his first book, "We are the same; it's the details that differ" in 2015 where he addressed behaviors and the motivation behind them.

Marcel Elfers developed a systematic approach to behavioral profiling through written communication. He integrates handwriting analysis, statement analysis[1], and behavioral trend analysis to come to reasonably accurate profiles. He changed careers to profiling services and Questioned Document Examination in 2010.

The case he is most proud of is assisting law enforcement in identifying the author of a pencil on tile written school threat (Elfers, School shooter 2018). His profiling triad method identified the author within a few hours, explained his motivation and what the troubled teenager looked like. The school principal was astonished about the accuracy of the description. The teenager was confronted and admitted to being the author of the threat. He volunteered to seek psychiatric assistance. This was the best possible outcome.

Marcel Elfers is available for behavioral profile consultations, threat assessments, and Questioned Document Examination.

---

[1] Statement Analysis is a Registered Trademark by Mark McClish

Accolades

"Marcel Elfers, your special gift is synthesizing information - you're amazing at it! Being clear, direct, concise. Economizing words, and saving your energy for the support and love I've seen you give mc and othcrs.

Teaching and explaining, in a way that to me has never sounded condescending. And finally, going straight to the heart of the matter, and seeing people for who they are, not their masks.

I'll never forget when that Type Three mask of mine was asking you for input and feedback on something impressive, I did. You were impressed the right amount, but you kept shifting the focus back to getting to know me, not my impressive outcomes.

This created a paradigm shift in me that immensely helped me understand myself, my childhood, and my other current relationships. I very much appreciate your friendship in this [Facebook] group, and I think you are wise and generous like an Enneagram Type Five is divinely purposed to be!" – D.G. 2016

September 27, 2012

To Whom it may concern:

It is my pleasure to introduce you to Marcel Elfers and his unique investigative skills. After inviting Marcel to my private on-line profiling group for the study of criminals, using the manual and system I developed, I became quickly aware of his innovative talents. He combines non-verbal behavioral clues, linguistic contextual analysis, and handwriting analysis to arrive at accurate character profiles.

During the time spent with the on-line group, he has presented his findings with detailed and innovative illustrations. He is observant, objective, and systematic in his approach. He builds a foundation for compelling conclusions regarding the behavioral characteristics of an author.

Marcel assisted with some of my cases and was able to add breadth to my approach and findings. He is a consummate professional who smoothly integrates his varied skills. He illuminates with a riveting insight into the hidden motivations and likely behavior of suspects or jurors.

His unique skill-set makes him an asset in security investigations and courtroom observations. His reports are understood by handwriting analysts, security professionals, law professionals, and laymen alike. I recommend Marcel Elfers for his expertise, professionalism, and detailed presentations.

Sincerely, Kimon S. Iannetta, author of "Danger Between The Lines".

February 2013

I have known Mr. Elfers for close to twenty years and have always been fascinated by his skill and expertise in handwriting analysis. I work in Superior Court for Snohomish County. Recently, I referred a matter to Mr. Elfers to gain his professional insight as to the level of threat a particular defendant posed toward his stalking victim. The only details I provided Mr. Elfers were the gender and approximate age of the person in question. To my amazement, Mr. Elfers' lengthy and detailed report outlined with impressive accuracy the known traits and characteristics of the defendant. Most impressive, however, was Mr. Elfers' skilled insight into the defendant's "pent up anger of a sexual nature." While this insight did not come as a surprise to me, it was troubling in nature as it confirmed my suspicions.

While this evidence is generally inadmissible in a court of law, it is a valuable tool in formulating a plan of attack, so to speak. I highly recommend, without reservation, Mr. Elfers for his expertise in forensic handwriting analysis.

D.H.

Contents

About the Author 6

Accolades 7

Suffer in silence 12

Author's note 13

The JonBenét case 18

Master Profiler through written communication 20

Deception 22

The 911 call 24

Boulder Police Department errors 30

Observations by Officers French and Arndt 32

The District Attorney Office 34

Team Ramsey 36

CNN interview 38

The coroner report 42

Staging 44

The Author 45

Statement Analysis 45

Handwriting comparison analysis 59

Steve Thomas 68

Glove 68

Mathematical probability 69

Handwriting analysis 72

Disguise 75

Patsy's behavior 78

Type Two 79

Emotional impact 83

Fabrication 88

No intruder 91

Motivation 98

John's behavior 98

Dictionary 103

Burke's behavior 108

What we know 112

The hidden message 116

Alibi building 121

A viable scenario 125

Patsy accidentally hit JonBenét 125

S.B.T.C [no period] 128

John's possible influence 132

Alternative theories 134

Mismanagement 139

Grand Jury 139

Exoneration 142

The final chapter 145

Summaries 151

Alleged intruder observations: 151

Patsy observations: 152

The final chapter

John observations: 153

Burke observations: 153

Deception tactics observed 154

Addendums 156

Ransom Note page 1 156

Ransom Note page 2 157

Ransom Note page 3 158

Coroner report page 1 159

Mary Lacy exoneration letter page 1 160

Mary Lacy exoneration letter page 2 161

Mary Lacy exoneration letter page 3 162

Bode technologies page 1 163

Body Technologies page 2 164

References 165

Bibliography 168

Suffer in silence

Through the veil

Peeks

The recipient …

Of the lie

Out of the darkness

Of blame

And shame

Carrying the heaviness

Of why?

- Nola Brown
Canadian Poet Extraordinaire

Author's note

Adults taking choice away from children, who do not even realize they have a choice, infuriates me. The most vulnerable age group is age three through eight-year-old children and this is when the vast majority of sexual abuse starts. A child losing their basic rights[2] at an early age learns to see themselves as objects, unwanted, and unloved.

The statistics on child molestation and sexual abuse are staggering. Research has shown about 60% of girls and 40% of boys are molested while about 1 in 5 girls and 1 in 12.5 boys are sexually abused before age 18 (Pereda 2009). The abuser is 95% of the time someone they know and trust (NAPCAN n.d.) with 90% of the perpetrators being male.

A six-year-old was sexually abused and she left her body to escape the pain. At age sixteen, she was married against her will to a 35-year-old man. She moved to the United States to get away from her family. Her erratic and demonstrative behavior was an ill attempt to hide her pain. A five-year-old girl was raped by her stepbrother. She had an out-of-body experience as well and saw two hands coming from the sky comforting her. Her relationship with God was permanently established at that moment. A young girl was physically, emotionally, and sexually abused from age five through sixteen. She had multiple out-of-body experiences including floating around and being abducted. Next to the abuse and out-of-body experiences, these women have the phrase, "Sometimes I do not know whether I am dreaming or whether it is real", in common.

The abuse typically continues into their teenage years until the moment he or she finds the courage to take their power back.

---

[2] The right to refuse, reject, request

And some, in utter desperation, do so with a gun. They were led to the edge of unthinkable violence, experienced another out-of-body event, lost control, and acted on it. They learned early to separate mind and body to negate the pain they were going through. Their ability to recall this stress-reaction may become habitual with their mind being an outsider looking in and their bodies on auto-pilot. In such instances, they are purely driven by self-preservation instinct.

It is no surprise that adults who experienced severe childhood abuse feel unsure of what they are capable of. They have been on the edge; they know what they are capable of, and with their minds critically detached do not feel in control. The vast majority become law-abiding citizens and do not wish to harm. They typically fear they may overstep boundaries again in stressful situations knowing they lose control. Some others are unable to control their impulses and become serial offenders.

The worst consequence of childhood abuse is psychological. The inability to ward off psychological intrusions, being dependent on an individual you know and trust, damages our self-image and self-worth. The realization we are vulnerable and at-risk imprints the need to self-protect.

Chronic victimization impacts our self-concept negatively. An unsuspecting child placed their trust in adults and being betrayed is a ramification for a lifetime of self-doubt, a false personal narrative, and a misconstrued worldview. They learn to not rely on others and shield their heart from betrayal and disappointment. They may not develop the full range of human emotions making it difficult to function in the world. Their negative internal dialogue is a constant: I am not worthy, I do not matter, I am unlovable, and I do not belong.

Extreme independence is a trauma response as a result of significant trust issues. The constant fear, enforced by perceived threats, is a mental trap. That fear closed doors and with every passing year, more doors are closed until nobody is allowed entry. A scarred and broken heart builds an impenetrable wall where nothing is let in, not even unconditional love and appreciation. Severe sexual, physical, and emotional abuse stuns emotional growth and often halts at the age where the emotional impact was the strongest.

Sexual abuse steals the sense you own your body and feels like, "I am valued for my physical being and not for who I am". Violation of our body develops a heightened sense of vulnerability while the lack of appreciation for who we are invalidates us. They are guarded and forced to live in the moment ready to react to real or perceived threats. Severely abused children are hypervigilant and perpetually in fight or flight mode. Eventually, their adulthood behavior reflects the environment they once lived in. Past chaos creates future chaos. Emotional dysregulation with an unstable self-image is often the end-product.

Children believe their circumstances are their choices and cannot phantom an abuser, cult leader, or provider normalized repulsive behaviors. As teens, they are detached from acceptable social standards, feel different, and believe they do not belong. As adults, they remain suspicious and apprehensive about mundane situations in anticipation of threats and chaos. Abused children may not figure out how to cope with their past and punish someone in the present. Intimates, partners, and lovers and those they are most comfortable with, are often the target. They lash out against the world instead of facing their abuser and take their power back.

Unresolved emotional issues tend to linger on and may exacerbate a downslide into mental illness. In severe cases, they may shut down their emotions, become socially isolated, and comfortably numb. Some resort to self-harm and risk-taking, like cutting and thrill-seeking, just to feel something. In the end, they repress their issues, suffer in silence, and project their pain into the world.

Fear feeds cognitive distortions permitting them to focus on and judge behavior instead of intent. Preoccupied with the expectation of being harmed, they live in the moment and do not appreciate the positive intentions of others. A fluctuating self-image allows for dramatic shifts in relationships, personal values, and goals. Self-protection evolves into keeping others at bay and pushing them away. The most mundane social situations are scrutinized and may trigger anxiety. Unexpected and unreasonable outbursts expose their struggle to trust and intrapsychic turmoil. Poor impulse control develops into violating other people's rights. They tend to be blind to the emotional impact they have on others and are oblivious to forcing others to go through their trauma with them. The now habitual, maladaptive, and obsessive-compulsive behaviors turn pathological and become a way of life.

In worst-case scenarios, emotional dysregulation and poor impulse control progress into disruptive relationships with secondary trauma as a consequence. Their suspicious nature evolves into intense and unstable relationships marked by vacillation between over-involvement and dismissal of an intimate. In these cases, their childhood abuse is easily recognized as their internal dialogue is expressed through major shifts in behavioral expression. They may reject genuine love and appreciation. To feel safe, they return to what they are familiar with: being on-guard, anticipating danger, and self-destructive behaviors. They punish their environment and feel they take control; however, they only project their pain onto others and force them to live through their pain with them. The rejection of kindness and love becomes a self-fulfilling prophecy: "I am unloved, unwanted, an object". They ask themselves, "why would anyone love me?" Sadly, true love and appreciation remain a foreign concept for them.

The final chapter

An abused and exploited child all too often receives a lifelong sentence with intra-psychic turmoil, inter-personal conflict, and deprivation. This way, the abuser's charade is passed on to the next generation by doing to others what was done to them. This is why I do not ask myself: "why are you this way?" I ask myself, "why would you not be this way?"

We need to keep in mind that, "it takes a village to raise a child" and equally, "it takes a village to conceal abuse". It is no wonder child abuse angers me to no end as I have been, like countless others, on the receiving end of that very mistrust, ominous fabrication, and gaslighting. Childhood abuse has a major, and above all, lasting effect on society as a whole.

The greatest gift a parent can give a child is self-worth. A child needs to learn to make sound independent choices. Nurturance gives a child personal value, affection, and reassurance while guidance provides direction, structure, and discipline. Parents determine the quality of future generations and societies.

In sum: We all have a cross to carry. Be kind. Be relevant.

I dedicate this book to childhood abuse survivors. You are heard, you are seen, and you are recognized. You were wronged, betrayed, and the blame lies squarely with the adults in the room. I wish to empower you by acknowledging that, "yes, you are enough".

- Marcel Elfers, QDE

The JonBenét case

JonBenét, affectionately called Jonni-B, was found dead in the basement of her own home. She was in full rigor mortis when discovered around 1 pm on December 26th, 1996. A two-and-a-half-page ransom note was left behind demanding $118,000 for the ~~delivery~~, eh …, pick-up of JonBenét. It made no sense to write a lengthy ransom note and leave the body behind.

My interest in the case peaked in 2007. At that time, I built a strong case for who wrote the ransom note, why the note was written, and what the message in the ransom note revealed. My observations and explanations of what happened that night were met with indifference by then Boulder Chief of Police Mark Beckner. A synopsis of the case can be found in my book, "We are the same; it's the details that differ" (2015).

I have hesitated for the longest time whether to document my findings on the JonBenét case in book form. I always felt justice would not be served providing the circumstances and the outcome of the case. It turned out inter-departmental strife and politics stood in the way of justice itself. Recently, a woman I love and admire, whose childhood story I know all too well, persuaded me to write my discoveries, insights, and conclusions down for the public to read. She commented, "It is validation for the horrors many abused children go through. This gives them a voice and possibly the courage to step forward".

The final chapter

The JonBenét case lingers on for a good reason. The intruder theory is illogical, does not match the evidence, and is absurd.

1. There was zero evidence an intruder was present.
2. Leaving JonBenét's body behind was illogical.
3. The Ramseys were minimally cooperative with law enforcement and aggressively shielded by their team of lawyers from the very beginning.
4. The Ramseys' behavior was unlike any parent concerned with finding the intruder turned killer.
5. The two-and-a-half-page ransom note, the 911 call, their interviews, their handwriting, as well as mirroring of the O.J. Simpson defense team tactics, all point to the Ramseys knowing what happened that night.

Steve Thomas, the lead investigator in the JonBenét murder case, did an excellent job. He was tenacious, obsessed with justice, and hunted for the truth. He discovered a massive amount of circumstantial evidence and, in my opinion, solved the case just to be stonewalled by the District Attorney Office.

Steve Thomas turned in his badge after 18 months of investigation and wrote a scathing resignation letter addressed to the Boulder Chief of Police Mark Beckner.

You, Mr. Steve Thomas, are the other reason why I am documenting my findings and theory about what happened that night. You deserve a medal for working the case hard and continued to do so even when you realized you were pushing water uphill only to get wet. I hope my conclusion to the case finds your way and that you will grin ear to ear when you read S.B.T.C [no period] is the logical conclusion of the hidden message in the ransom note. So, here it is. My journey through a labyrinth of misdeeds, misspellings, misdirection, and making sense of it all.

Master Profiler through written communication

I received certification as a Trial Run Master Profiler in 2010 with an emphasis on criminality. Over time, I added Statement Analysis and Behavioral Trend Analysis. This multifaceted profiling triad provides more accurate results than using stand-alone disciplines. Lastly, recognizing the emotional impact on handwriting behavior is crucial to understand the emotional status of an author.

What the profiling triad can do for you:
- Handwriting analysis can reveal major behavioral characteristics of the ransom note author.
    - The author was highly anxious.
    - The author is prone to kindness.
    - The author is empathetic.
- The emotional connection to a sentence or just a word can reveal the impact it has on the author.
    - The author was emotionally attached to the victim.
- Statement Analysis can reveal the lens of perspective.
    - The author knew John intimately.
    - The author coerced John.
    - The author is probably a female.
- Statement Analysis can reveal deception, disguise, and evasion.
    - What we talk about is important enough to mention.
    - The author was building an alibi.
- Behavioral trends reveal a distinct pattern.
    - Behavioral patterns are driven by a core motivation established in our childhood.
    - The author's core is being good to others, being needed, and earning appreciation.

The final chapter

In this book, I built the case based on the evidence available. My goal is to show how facts and circumstantial evidence fit together pointing to one, and only one, logical conclusion:

1. Handwriting analysis reveals Patsy wrote the ransom note.
2. Statement Analysis reveals John probably assisted in authoring the ransom note.
3. The ransom note owns elements of alibi building:
   a. Bring an adequate size attache to the bank.
   b. You will also be denied her remains.
4. S.B.T.C [no period] characteristics:
   a. The lack of period means non-habitual acronym use.
   b. The hidden message suggests the acronym is the conclusion of the ransom note.
5. The intruder theory was and is absurd.
6. The crime scene was staged beyond a reasonable doubt.

The above are great clarity statements and represent a strong opinion. The case will be presented in an abstract, logical, and methodical manner. Understanding is based on clarity and for that reason superfluous and distracting information is limited.

"The evolution of truth is towards simplicity".

In the end, Occam's Razor prevails.

Deception

Every good lie has a little bit of truth and repetition normalizes alternative facts. Deception is the attempt to cause someone to believe a falsehood to gain an advantage. In my observations, mentally unhealthy individuals with a need to defend their egos and those who protect themselves through misrepresentation, tend to have the same agenda and tactics. They distort reality, create chaos, blame others, evade, and aim to avoid responsibility being unable to cope. They provide, repeat, and enforce erroneous conclusions providing a falsehood to convince others. A brief introduction to common deception principles is important to follow the JonBenét case.

1. Baseline
   a. The most important principle is to establish how someone habitually writes, behaves, and speaks. Deviation from an established baseline is a red flag.
2. Word selection
   a. A change in a word is a change in reality. Every word has an emotional value and a change increases or decreases the emotional value.
3. Downplaying
   a. People responsible do not want to see themselves in a bad light and tend to use euphemisms.
4. Exaggeration
   a. People exaggerate to convince others.
5. Gaslighting
   a. Destabilizing a person by making them question their memory, perception, and judgment while using contradiction, denial, and belittlement.
6. Freudian slips
   a. A word or phrase revealing hidden experiences, motives, or wishes.

7. Deflection

      a. Changing subjects to shift attention away from yourself.
8. Evasion
      a. The act of telling a truth without divulging critical details.
9. Changes in recollection
      a. A person who experienced an event was in it with all five senses. We link memories to visuals, hearing, smells, taste, and touch. Our senses help us keep a storyline straight. Substantial changes in our recollection of an event suggest the event was not experienced.

The Ramseys were no different and used many deception strategies. Patsy as a major in journalism understood the power of communication, manipulating public opinion, and using the media to spread misinformation.

The intruder theory is implausible. A non-criminal wrote the two-and-a-half-page ransom note and the anonymous pedophile ring phone call diverted attention away from the Ramseys.

This is their story as told by the author of the ransom note.

The 911 call

Patsy Ramsey called 911 on December 26th, 1996; this is our starting point. A caller needs an immediate response for assistance. The caller has control over the narrative and the information they provide. In other words, "what" they say and "how" they say it directly influences the emergency urgency response as well as the form their assistance will take.

Every word has a certain emotional value to the speaker and is a direct expression of their perspective. An important principle needs to be addressed before we look at the transcript of the 911 call. Rule number one of the rules of engagement is:

We talk about what is most important to us first.

This principle is the most important in the rules of engagement and one of the many ways we expose ourselves. What we may consider a trivial comment was apparently important enough for the speaker to mention. A friend of mine texted me; "How was New York?" I replied, "NY is coming up in May; I am preparing the presentation right now." She texted back: "Fun! You will be on the other side of the States. One end to the other end!"

Again, every word has an emotional value to the speaker, and that is why I do not ask myself, "Why mention the obvious?" I ask myself, "Why is this important enough for you to mention?"

It turns out my friend drove cross country from Montana to South Carolina two weeks prior to the text. The comment reflected on her own recent experience. Remember, what is trivial to you has significance to the speaker. And therefore,

People say exactly what they mean.

The Ramseys behaved suspiciously from the very first words Patsy uttered in her 911 call at 5:52 am. The call is our first contact where she volunteered her perspective. Pay attention to the flow of information and the linguistic character of what is said. Here we go: (underline added).

1. Patsy Ramsey (PR): (inaudible) police
2. 911: (inaudible)
3. PR: 755 Fifteenth Street
4. 911: What's going on ma'am?
5. PR: We have a kidnapping … Hurry Please
6. 911: Explain to me what is going on, ok?
7. PR: We have a … There is a note left and our daughter is gone
8. 911: A note was left and your daughter is gone?
9. PR: Yes
10. 911: How old is your daughter?
11. PR: She is six years old; she is blonde … six years old
12. 911: How long ago was this?
13. PR: I don't know. Just found a note … a note and my daughter is missing
14. 911: Does it say who took her?
15. PR: What?
16. 911: Does it say who took her?
17. PR: No, I don't know it's there … there's a ransom note
18. 911: It's a ransom note?
19. PR: It says S.B.T.C Victory …. Please
20. 911: Ok, what's your name? Are you...
21. PR: Patsy Ramsey...I am the mother. Oh my God. Please.
22. 911: I'm...Ok, I'm sending an officer over, ok?
23. PR: Please.
24. 911: Do you know how long she's been gone?
25. PR: No, I don't, please, we just got up and she's not here. Oh my God Please.
26. 911: Ok.

Line 3. Patsy provided her address first prioritizing location above the kidnapped JonBenét. This makes the address her starting point. The home is where it is happening and JonBenét would be found in the home as we know in hindsight.

Line 5. Patsy continued with, "We have a kidnapping" which does not create urgency. The word "a" is non-descriptive as this includes the kidnapping of your pet. A well-defined statement would be, "My daughter has been kidnapped!!" Short, to the point, and creates urgency for the responders.

Line 5. The word "We" alludes to the parents and shows her perspective is about them above JonBenét. We would expect, "my daughter has been kidnapped" and that would make JonBenét the subject of the call. Incidentally, the word "We" is often instinctively used when someone wants or needs to share guilt to reduce personal responsibility.

Line 5. The word selection "a" is impersonal and implies emotional distancing providing the dire circumstances.

These first statements raise suspicion since Patsy left out critical information needed to create urgency. We expect direct and blunt language to prod law enforcement into action. Kim Archuletta, the 911 operator, would later say, "the call seemed rehearsed".

Line 7. We have a ....is an unfinished sentence and likely a repeat of line 5 suggesting she picked up a rehearsed script where she left off after being interrupted by line 6.

Line 7. ... There is a note left and our daughter is gone. The use of "We" (5) and "our" involves more than one person. We can argue it is appropriate as there are two parents involved. However, it is curious from the perspective that the bond between mother and daughter is the strongest. The word "our" seems to go against maternal instinct. The use of "my" daughter would have been a stronger statement.

Line 7. The use of "a" note remains unspecified.

Line 7. Subconsciously, Patsy might have accidentally leaked she knew JonBenét was already dead with the word selection "gone". Gone implies not to be found and completely lost. In the case of a person, it may refer to death. This observation is consistent with the emotional impact we will see in the handwriting.

Line 11. She is blonde … six years old. Patsy is providing more information than asked for and may need to convince.

Linc 13. Thc Pcrsonal Pronoun I is missing in "Just found a notc". The lack of a PPI suggests the speaker does not want to own the statement, distanced herself from that statement, and is another marker for potential deception.

Line 13. "Our daughter" (7) changed to "my daughter". A change in a word is a change in reality. Although "my" daughter is more realistic given the situation, the use of "a" note still does not explain it is a ransom note.

Line 13. "Gone" (7) changed to "missing" ... My interpretation is the word "gone" was used to reflect on what she already knew. JonBenét was "gone forever". This leakage makes sense as their coverup just started and anxiety ran high initially. As the call progressed, Patsy calmed down a little and fell back on her rehearsed storyline. Now the child was just "missing" implying misplaced and to be found. This is a correction in her intended perspective to maintain the illusion of a kidnapping.

So far, Patsy did not create the expected urgency and had a change in her reality from "gone" to "missing". This suggests fabrication and she did not live the situation. So far, the call raises questions and we are without any significant conclusion.

Line 15. To answer a question with a question is stalling for time to gain time to think about what to say. Reduced spontaneity is a marker for deception.

Line 17. The note's intent is now revealed. It is a "ransom note" and even the operator is surprised by the change. Patsy knew the content of the note and why not say that immediately?

The fact Patsy upped the ante by finally mentioning it is actually a ransom note reveals there was no initial urgency by revealing the true nature of the call. An authentic caller would say "My daughter is missing. We have a ransom note" right from the start.

Line 19. We are well into the conversation and Patsy brings up the last two words of the ransom note. This does not mean she would have read the whole ransom note however the rule "we talk about what is important to us" applies. There was a significant need to mention S.B.T.C [no period].

Line 25. "We just got up" is information not asked for and implies Patsy wanted to make sure law enforcement knew they were asleep before finding the note. This may be part of alibi-building.

Patsy hung up on the 911 operator and disconnected with the only source that could provide her help. The cradle did not drop properly on the wall unit. Voices were heard after she hung up. It was difficult to decipher but the Aero Space Corporation in Los Angeles did their best and reported they heard Patsy saying, "help me, Jesus". In the background Burke, their almost 10-year-old son, was heard saying, "what did you find?" and John appears to have said, "we are not talking to you".

The makers of "The Case of JonBenet Ramsey" hired an audio engineer to enhance the recordings and unearth what, if anything, was said after Patsy hung up and found similar results.

John and Patsy claimed Burke stayed in bed the whole time. The evidence, despite being questionable, shows us otherwise. The inquisitive Burke would not stay in bed the whole time with all the commotion in the home. If Burke asked that question then he likely did not know what happened. A 10-year-old would know the implication of JonBenét's death if he was the cause. He would be cowering in his room hiding underneath his blankets. Burke's behavior did not match the behavior of a guilty child.

Again, we talk about what is most important to us first. The need to mention S.B.T.C [sic] demonstrates its relative importance to Patsy. The question is "why was this important enough for her to mention?" We will find out the meaning is the natural conclusion of the fabricated narrative.

The distancing language implies a need to avoid the situation because it is too difficult emotionally. The use of *ransom note* shows us she knew the content while first using *a note* reveals Patsy did not pursue urgency. This is not a parent looking for assistance to find her missing daughter. As a rule, callers who do not ask for assistance for the victim immediately or ask assistance for themselves are guilty, involved, or know what happened. The 911 call is without a doubt deceptive. It has elements Patsy knew what happened and alibi building.

JonBenét was found in the basement seven hours after the 911 call at 5:52 am The Ramseys lawyered up around 7:30 am and were minimally cooperative with law enforcement. Their team of lawyers, soon to be dubbed, "Team Ramsey", shielded them immediately from questions and interviews. The Ramseys knew law enforcement needed to ask them questions and obtain biological samples to eliminate them as suspects. They chose to hide behind a wall of lawyers instead. Again, the parents had no urgency to solve the kidnapping. Why? What happened?

In sum:
Patsy did not prioritize her daughter and had no authentic urgency. The call seemed planned and rehearsed. John and Patsy claimed Burke slept through it all, yet, he appears to talk on the 911 tape.

Boulder Police Department errors

There is no doubt the Boulder Police Department made major mistakes. They were short-staffed on Christmas day and inexperienced in murder cases in Boulder, Colorado.

Officer Rick French arrived in his black-and-white squad car within 3-4 minutes after the 911 call. This was a potential mistake as kidnappers may monitor the home for police involvement. Of course, he did not know what was going on. A bigger mistake was not sealing off the whole home and yard as it was a crime scene.

The Ramseys immediately contacted friends after the 911 call and the home was soon invaded by many people moving around freely. The crime scene was soon compromised and contaminated. Some of the people present during the day were:

1. John, Patsy, and Burke Ramsey
2. Fleet and Priscilla White (neighbors)
3. John and Barbara Fernie (neighbors)
4. First responder Officer Rick French
5. Paul Reichenbach, patrol supervisor Boulder Police Department
6. Detective Linda Arndt
7. Reverend Rol Hoverstock
8. Two technicians
9. Two victim advocates

A fingerprinting technician was dusting for prints and was followed by a victim advocate cleaning up after the dusting with a spray bottle in hand. Another technician took photographs of the ransom note but not in the location where it was originally found. The ransom note was moved.

The unfortunate Detective Linda Arndt was later left alone to supervise seven adults that were able to move around at will inside the home. She was unable to control the number of people. She was instructed to use radio silence in case the kidnappers were using police scanners. Her cell phone calls for assistance were unsuccessful and she remained by herself on the scene.

Detective Arndt noticed John was missing and estimated the time frame to be from about 11 am to noon. At around 1 pm, she made a poor judgment call by instructing two civilians, John Ramsey and Fleet White, his neighbor, to search the home from top to bottom and to leave the evidence in place. John Ramsey beelined to the basement and almost immediately found JonBenét's body in a small and obscure little room soon nicknamed the "wine cellar". Instead of following instructions, John Ramsey pulled the duct tape off her mouth and brought her tiny body, already in full rigor mortis, upstairs. He placed her on the floor per Detective Arndt's instructions. The next mistake for Detective Arndt was to move the body to a rug by the Christmas tree. John Ramsey threw a blanket over her body before Detective Arndt could stop him. Someone covered JonBenét's feet with a gray sweatshirt.

The Boulder Police Department did not collect the clothing of John and Patsy Ramsey to eliminate them as suspects. As we will later learn, it would take a year before the Ramseys finally provided the clothing they wore just to find out that four fibers of Patsy's jacket were stuck under the duct tape placed over JonBenét's mouth. That was an interesting find because one fiber may be accidentally picked up. But four fibers suggest Patsy's jacket was close and Patsy was likely in it. I imagine she was tearing the duct tape and touched her jacket with the glue side of the tape.

Observations by Officers French and Arndt

Officer Rick French was the first to arrive on the scene. Patsy opened the door wearing black pants and a red turtleneck. He noticed her hair and make-up were intact. This observation became very important as investigators later discovered Patsy was wearing the same clothing the day before. And since she stated in her 911 call, "we just got up" at 5:30, it is odd her hair and make-up were intact. It is a logical conclusion Patsy did not go to bed that night.

Officer Rick French walked through the house and the basement. He saw the little room where JonBenét was found later in the day. The door was closed and latched on the outside. He was looking for an escape route with an intruder in mind and did not open the door. Obviously, the intruder could not go into the room and latch the door on the outside. When he got back upstairs, he noticed Patsy "eyeballing" him through her fingers.
The Officer soon thought the behavior of the Ramseys was inconsistent with panicked parents in dire need of assistance to find their daughter. Officer French told Department Sergeant and Patrol Supervisor Paul Reichenbach, "something is not right".

Officer French would later feel guilty about not having opened that door. In hindsight, he may have found the body. On the other hand, John Ramsey may have moved her body to the little room during the time he was missing. If he had opened the door and she was not there and found later in the same little room, that could only mean the suspect was in the house with Detective Arndt.

Detective Arndt had her eyes wide open as well. John Ramsey discovered the body and brought her upstairs. She checked for a pulse and noticed the odor of decay. John Ramsey and Detective Arndt leaned over the body and she observed John Ramsey crying without tears. They locked eyes for a moment and Detective Arndt stated later "I knew he knew what happened".

She also noticed the two parents did not console each other. John Ramsey stayed in the den while Patsy remained on the couch in the sunroom. It was as if they were two disconnected individuals with separate agendas.

Fleet White, the neighbor, ran upstairs when John Ramsey found JonBenét. Fleet White dialed the phone not even realizing police were present. He created a lot of commotion yet Patsy stayed on her couch. She was physically brought to the body by her friends Priscilla White and Barbara Fernie. Patsy then threw herself over JonBenét's body adding more fibers as John did.

In sum:
1. Officer Rick French noticed Patsy dressed with hair and makeup intact.
2. Officer Rick French believed something was not right based on the behaviors of the parents.
3. Officer Rick French noticed Patsy eyeballing him.
4. Detective Arndt believed John knew what happened.
5. Detective Arndt noticed the parents did not console each other.
6. Detective Arndt noted Patsy did not come out of the sunroom when JonBenét's body was brought upstairs.

The crime scene was compromised and contaminated making the investigation more elaborate and difficult as far as the elimination of suspects was concerned. However, these mistakes turned out to be nothing compared to the handling of the case by the District Attorney's office.

The District Attorney Office

Alex Hunter was the Boulder County District Attorney since 1972 and entrenched in the political landscape in 1996. In essence, over time District Attorney Hunter became powerful in his position. He was deeply rooted with the power players in his district and developed a position where he was "the only game in town".

The District Attorney's Modus Operandi was to consistently plea-bargain to the point where plea-bargaining evolved into "pre-charging negotiations" between prosecutors and defense attorneys *before* the defendant was charged (Thomas 2000)[3]. The consequence of not seeing the inside of a courtroom is the quality of plea-bargaining increased. The lack of prosecution experience dwindled the quality of their courtroom skills.

There were 23 murder cases filed between 1992 and 1996 in Boulder County and none went to trial. The fact the Ramsey case did not see the courtroom would not come as a surprise. The District Attorney office simply did not take an aggressive stance and defense attorneys loved it.

There are two types of mistakes in life. There are unintentional mistakes and there are intentional mistakes. The Boulder Police Department made unintentional mistakes secondary to inexperience and these can be forgiven. Such mistakes reveal incompetence and are without intent.

The District Attorney Office made intentional mistakes in a progressive pattern by stonewalling the investigators, demanding proof beyond a reasonable doubt, reportedly leaking information, and using a tabloid reporter to influence the media. The tabloid reporter, Jeff Shapiro, had the home phone number of District Attorney Alex Hunter on speed dial. He claimed to talk with Alex Hunter on a daily basis and sometimes for hours at a time.

---

[3] Page 101

The final chapter

The role the District Attorney Office played in the JonBenét Ramsey case was significant and, in my opinion, far outweighed the mistakes Boulder Police Department made. The District Attorney Office virtually single-handedly decided the outcome of the case and disregarded mountains of circumstantial evidence any other defendant in any other district would be sent to prison.

The District Attorney Office was so used to negotiations outside the courtroom, that they developed a cozy, actually a too cozy, relationship with the defense team of the Ramseys. The most interesting and damning part of the relationship between team Ramsey and the District Attorney Office is that team Ramsey demanded the same privileges charged suspects receive. This included sharing pre-trial discovery or the sharing of information privy to investigators and the prosecution team. Discovery is normally shared with charged suspects only as they have the right to defend themselves based on the information gathered.

The District Attorney Office obliged and District Attorney Alex Hunter was the one who refused to charge the Ramseys in the first place. Yet, he gave them the same privileges as if they were charged. Needless to say, the investigative team was appalled, angry, and felt undermined.

Bill Hagmaier, head of the FBI's Child Abduction and Serial Killer Unit, asked District Attorney Hunter at one point in time; "No disrespect intended, Mister Hunter, but is this grand jury your call?" Hunter replied that he would work with his trusted advisers to reach a decision. Hagmaier pushed until Hunter admitted that the final decision would indeed be his. Hagmaier continued, "A little girl is moldering in the ground, and she shouldn't be. If the parents are involved, Mister Hunter, something needs to be done."

"This is a political decision," Hunter said. "I have to get with my people". The decision to move forward was apparently not based on evidence and justice rather it was "political". In my opinion, the tactics of this District Attorney Office should be subject to an investigation regarding obstruction of justice. Although I can understand the need for solid evidence, I do not understand negating the enormous amount of circumstantial evidence, denying a Grand Jury their recommendation while knowing the intruder theory is demonstrably false.

In sum:
The District Attorney Office has been using plea bargains habitually and developed a cozy relationship with the Ramsey defense team.

Team Ramsey

It is curious how quickly the Ramseys lawyered up. Patsy called 911 at 5:52 am and they lawyered up by 7:30 am.

Fleet White was one of the first neighbors at the Ramsey home. He told investigators later Mike Bynum, a team Ramsey lawyer, had called him and his wife shortly after the body was found at 1:05 pm. Fleet White revealed the Ramsey attorneys were already busy talking to witnesses on the afternoon of December 26th. John Ramsey explained in their book, "the death of innocence", that one of his friends recommended to lawyer up because parents are automatically suspect. Although this makes sense in a way, it does not explain their minimal cooperation that morning nor the lack of urgency to find the kidnapper of JonBenét.
The Ramseys were not charged, nor accused, not even suspects yet. They decided to lawyer up virtually immediately and hide behind a security wall. Without a doubt, they understood cooperation with the detectives was paramount to find the killer of JonBenét. It was their choice not to cooperate.

The O.J. Simpson trial was a media circus in 1995. This trial not only showed the strong influence of the media but also how his defense team loaded up the prosecutors with all kinds of theories and delay tactics to have the jury sit in court for 265 days. Team Ramsey mimicked the O.J. Simpson defense tactics likely with the input of Patsy who majored in Journalism.

One way to keep investigators busy and preoccupied was to accuse many people like their housemaid, neighbors, friends, disgruntled employees, and anyone within their social circle who visited the house over time. The tactic was to overload the prosecutors with nonsense leads to create confusion and wear the prosecutors out.

Team Ramsey played their cards well. They took the lead in demands and would not allow the Ramseys to be interviewed. The District Attorney Office, predisposed to plea-bargains, was in full-on pre-charging negotiations mode. Team Ramsey demanded the same privileges as a charged suspect would. And the "only game in town" effectively rolled over on his back like a puppy wanting to be scratched. The question is "why?"

The Ramseys were minimally cooperative and avoided investigators like the plague. Then, and seemingly out of the blue, the Ramseys made a strategic move. They agreed to a nationally televised CNN interview on January 1st, 1997.

In sum:
Team Ramsey shielded the Ramseys from the start. They applied the same tactics as the O.J. Simpson defense team the year before. They used the media to taint a potential jury pool.

CNN interview

Patsy had a degree in Journalism and did everything Texas Style. The nation just experienced the O.J. Simpson trial the year before. Patsy was fully aware of what role the media could play for them. A nationwide interview with Brian Cabell was the perfect tool.

Cabell: Why did you decide you wanted to talk now?
John Ramsey: "Well, we have been pretty isolated -- totally isolated -- for the last five days, but we've sensed from our friends that this tragedy has touched not just ourselves and our friends but many people. And we know that there's many people that are praying for us, that are grieving with us. And we want to thank them, to let them know that we are healing, and that we know in our hearts that JonBenét is safe and with God and that the grieving that we all have to do is for ourselves and for our loss, but we want to thank those people that care about us".

A theme is emerging. Finding the killer of their daughter is not a priority. The word *"Well"* stalls for time and often used to think about a rehearsed statement. John Ramsey is reflecting on everyone else, their prayers, the healing they need to do, and thanked them all. Although he said they were *totally isolated*, they were apparently in contact with *friends.*
I would expect him to look straight into the camera and say: "We are here to make clear to you, the murderer of my JonBenét, we will be moving heaven and earth to find you. If the public knows anything, hears anything, please help us bring justice for my daughter, JonBenét. Call the police hotline at (123) 456-7890"

Again, we talk about what is important to us first. Thanking the people praying for them had priority over finding his daughter. There was no urgency on John's part and matched Patsy's lack of urgency in the 911 call. They both knew what happened.
The word "tragedy" is very interesting exposing his perspective. John downplayed the murder of his child to a tragedy. A car

accident is tragic. The murder of his daughter through strangulation with a garrote made from items found in the basement is willful and involved active planning. The use of "tragedy" for the deliberate murder of your six-year-old daughter is downplaying the incident from intentional to accidental. A tragedy suggests a lack of intent and the strangulation shows willful and deliberate intent. The downplaying of the event makes sense from the perspective when you are the killer or your wife for that matter. You do not want to see yourself as a "murderer".

John Ramsey used the word "tragedy" repeatedly and made the claim, "it was a sexual predator and there is nothing logical in this … [pause]… tragedy" (investigation. 2000). The long pause before the word tragedy suggests he was looking for a word or was reevaluating what he just said.

It is very odd how John described the case as in, "nothing is logical" making the intruder "deranged" in his words. According to John, the intruder had a key and roamed the home while they were celebrating Christmas. The intruder then found pay stubs with his deferred payment of $118,000 and waited for all of them to go to bed. The intruder as described by John must be pretty intelligent, logical, and collected in his actions. And yes, there is nothing logical indeed in the explanation of what happened, that is. The claim it was a sexual predator is interesting as an easy scapegoat. Pageants are rife with elements objectifying women for their beauty.

The foundation of the intruder theory is not only weak; it is also based on unreasonable and increasingly unlikely events. The explanation a stranger was in the home defies all logic. This theory is stitched together to fit a false narrative only the esoteric would believe in their conviction the parents could not possibly have done this. I like to remind you filicide happens. Andrea Yates, Susan Smith, and Chris Watts come to mind.

After Patsy commented about how overwhelmed they were, John continued with; "But the other -- the other reason is that -- for our grief to resolve itself we now have to find out <u>why</u> this happened. This -- we cannot go on until we know <u>why</u>. <u>There is no answer</u> as to <u>why</u> our daughter died".

John prioritized "why" this happened instead of asking "what happened?" and "how did it happen?" Why it happened reflects on the motivation behind the event. What and how may lead to finding the murderer of his child. His primary interest in "why" it happened suggests he already knew what happened but does not understand the "why". The combination of "why this happened" and downplaying the murder to "this tragedy" show they knew what happened and there was no intent to kill their daughter. The word "tragedy" implies it was indeed an accident and downplaying a willful act to reduce feelings of guilt and responsibility. Ergo, the Ramseys were involved.

We know the blow to JonBenét's head came first and that blow was likely accidental. The word selection of the word "why" supports the idea there was no intent. When you kill with intent, you know why you killed and you do not ask why it happened. The phrasing "There is no answer" suggests to not look for an answer because you cannot find an answer that does not exist. This leakage furthers the idea there was no intruder and it was an accident. Like the 911 call, John and Patsy prioritized their own needs over finding the murderer of JonBenét. A pattern established itself in the first five days. It started with the 911 call and continued its pattern in the CNN interview.

Months later, John and Patsy played the media again with lawyers standing by to prevent asking key questions regarding JonBenét's death. Steve Thomas (Thomas 2000)[4] asked himself why any self-respecting journalist would even attend this charade when the tough and crime-solving questions cannot be asked. Despite this,

---

[4] Page 178

an interesting tidbit came out of that interview. John stated, "We will find you; I have that as the sole mission <u>for the rest of my life</u>" The word selection tells us he does not expect the murderer to be found otherwise "for the rest of my life" would not be within your expectation pattern. He revealed he did not expect the killer to be found soon. Not tomorrow, nor next week, nor next month, or within a few years. "For the rest of my life" is telling. Again, this supports the idea there was no intruder. As we can see, John's perspective leaks through over and over again.

The phrasing, "for the rest of my life" is loaded and a virtual bombshell in Statement Analysis. John is telling the world, openly and publicly that, "There is no answer", and the sentence, "sole mission for the rest of my life" implies John would never find the killer. When people reveal themselves, believe them.

In sum:
1. The 911 call is deceptive.
2. Law enforcement senses something is amiss.
3. John and Patsy hide behind a wall of lawyers
4. District Attorney Office stonewalls investigators.
5. John and Patsy chose media over law enforcement assistance
6. John's perspective is
   a. There is no answer to why it happened
   b. There is no intruder to be caught

The Ramseys prioritizing the media to maintain their image is not in line with grieving parents in desperate search of the murderer.

The coroner report

FINAL DIAGNOSIS:

I. Ligature strangulation.

A. Circumferential ligature with associated ligature furrow of neck.

B. Abrasions and petechial hemorrhages neck.

C. Petechial hemorrhages, conjunctival surfaces of eyes and skin of face.

II. Cranio-cerebral injuries.

A. Scalp contusion.

B. Linear, comminuted fracture of right side of skull.

C. Linear pattern of contusions of right cerebral hemisphere.

D. Subarachnoid and subdural hemorrhage.

E. Small contusions, tips of temporal lobes.

III. Abrasion of right cheek.

IV. Abrasion/contusion, posterior right shoulder.

V. Abrasions of left lower back and posterior left lower leg.

VI. Abrasion and vascular congestion of vaginal mucosa.

VII. Ligature of right wrist.

John E. Meyer performed the autopsy on December 27th, 1996 at 8:15 am. His conclusion reads as follows:

CLINICOPATHOLOGIC CORRELATION: Cause of death of this six-year-old female is asphyxia by strangulation associated with craniocerebral trauma.

JonBenét's demise was caused by a blow to her head leaving an 8.5-inch skull fracture and strangulation. The skull fracture was in the shape of a Maglite and may be linked to the Maglite found in the kitchen which appeared to have been wiped clean. Dr. Werner Spitz tested the shape of the crack on the skull by hitting a cadaver with such a flashlight. The shape matched and JonBenét's skull fracture was probably caused by the Maglite blow.

The final chapter

The autopsy reported petechia on the neck around the garrote cord and the eyelids. Petechia are little red dots or spots caused by blood leaking out of burst capillaries. And this suggests JonBenét's heart was beating building up pressure around the cord breaking the blood vessels.

The petechia and duct tape suggests the blow to the head came likely first. The perfect lip prints on the duct tape mean JonBenét was not fighting the tape. The duct tape was not needed as she was unconscious already. It was determined the strangulation came 45 minutes to two hours after the blow to the head according to the level of brain swelling. Cyril Wecht, another renowned coroner, made a presentation stating the strangulation came first because the bleeding from the skull fracture was minimal for the injury. Again, she would have been dead and the duct tape would still not be necessary.

Regardless of the sequence of events, John Ramsey found JonBenét and pulled duct tape from her mouth which contained "perfect lip prints" on the glue side. The child was not fighting the duct tape and was unconscious before the tape was placed.

Another interesting autopsy finding is regarding her vagina. "Vaginal Mucosa: All of the sections contain vascular congestion and focal interstitial chronic inflammation". A panel of pediatric experts determined JonBenét suffered chronic vaginal trauma before the day she was killed. Second, her hymen was compromised. The experts could not come to agreement regarding the cause of the damage. She could have been sexually abused but other causes are also possible including rough cleaning by a frustrated parent.

Staging

It has been widely reported and recognized by the FBI the crime scene was staged and performed by an unsophisticated killer.

Her lifeless body was found in a little room in the basement. A room that was more or less difficult to find. Her body was wrapped in a blanket. A garrote was placed around her neck and her arms were above her head when she was found in full rigor mortis. The loosely tied cord around her wrists above her head appears to be a vague attempt to make it look like she was tied up. It is entirely possible her body was in full or partial rigor mortis when the staging occurred and her arms could not be moved into a position behind her back. The blanket wrapped around her body suggests a caring attitude towards the child. The garrote knot was placed on the back of the neck implying the offender could not face the child. The staging suggests it was the work of someone who was emotionally attached to the victim; like a parent.

Besides the above damning observations, duct tape was placed on her mouth. After John removed it, investigators noted a perfect lip print on the glue side of duct tape. The child did not try to remove the tape and implies she was at minimum unconscious or had already passed when the duct tape was placed. An intruder would place duct tape to keep a child quiet. This was obviously unnecessary from the kidnapper's perspective.

In sum:

The two opposing coroner points of view are a distinction without a difference. The child was unconscious when the duct tape was placed and tells us the crime scene was staged. JonBenét also had chronic vaginal inflammation.

The Author

Statement Analysis

The ransom note is the most important piece of evidence. The two and half pages long and rambling at best provided a wealth of information.

Page 1
1. Mr. Ramsey.
2. Listen carefully! We are a
3. group of individuals that represent
4. a small foreign faction. We don't
5. respect your bussiness [sic] but not the
6. country that it serves. At this
7. time we have your daughter in our
8. posession [sic]. She is safe and un harmed
9. and if you want her to see 1997,
10. you must follow our instructions to
11. the letter.
12. You will withdraw $118,000.00
13. from your account. $100,000 will be
14. in $100 bills and the remaining
15. $18,000 in $20 bills. Make sure
16. that you bring an adequate size
17. attache to the bank. When you
18. get home you will put the money
19. in a brown paper bag. I will
20. call you between 8 and 10 am
21. tomorrow to instruct you on delivery.
22. The delivery will be exhausting so
23. I advise you to be rested. If
24. we monitor you getting the money
25. early, we might call you early to
26. arrange an earlier delivery of the

Page 2:
27. money and hence a [sic]earlier
28. delivery pickup of your daughter.
29. Any deviation of my instructions
30. will result in the immediate
31. execution of your daughter. You
32. will also be denied her remains
33. for proper burial. The two
34. gentlemen watching over your daughter
35. do \not/ particularly like you so I
36. advise you not to provoke them.
37. Speaking to anyone about your
38. situation, such as Police, F.B.I., etc.
39. will result in your daughter being
40. beheaded. If we catch you talking
41. to a stray dog, she dies.
42. If you alert bank authorities, she dies.
43. If the money is in any way
44. marked or tampered with, she
45. dies. You will be scanned for
46. electronic devices and if any are
47. found, she dies. You can try to
48. deceive us but be warned that
49. we are familiar with law enforcement
50. countermeasures and tactics. You
51. stand a 99% chance of killing
52. your daughter if you try to out
53. smart us. Follow our instructions
Page 3:
54. and you stand a 100% chance
55. of getting her back. You and your family
56. are under constant
57. scrutiny as well as the authorities.
58. Don't try to grow a brain
59. John. You are not the only

60. fat cat around so don't think
61. that killing will be difficult.
62. Don't underestimate us John.
63. Use that good Southern common
64. sense of yours. It is up to
65. you now John!
66.   Victory!
67. S.B.T.C

Statement analysis explains we talk about what is important enough to mention and every word expressed represents part of the speaker's perspective. Words have meaning and emotional significance to the speaker or writer for that matter. People tend to say what is important or what they relate to the most first. People always talk from their perspective even when they talk about others. When you are asked, "what do you love about your best friend?" you tend to answer with what you relate to the most regarding your friend. This is in essence your personal penchant or perspective projected onto your friend. You either own or wished you owned what you admire about your friend. And, people find it a lot easier to compliment others relative to self-promotion.

The ransom note is the crucial piece of evidence and contains the answers we are looking for. It is a blessing the ransom note is two-and-a-half-pages long providing investigators a lot to work with. John and Patsy claimed an intruder had come into the home and kidnapped their daughter. The circumstances, the handwriting, the word selection, and the hidden message tell us otherwise. Second, trial notes were found and one started with "Mr. and Mrs. I". The "I" is assumed to be the stem of the /R of Ramsey. Pam Griffin, one of Patsy's friends, would later tell investigators Patsy admitted she was the author of the "Mr. and Mrs. I" note.

Perspective is everything in Statement Analysis. An unusual perspective not befitting the context often reveals a hidden meaning, a coverup, fabrication, or a lie. Investigators soon discovered the ransom note was written in the home with a sharpie belonging to the Ramseys. The Sharpie was placed back in its canister. Tear marks of the ransom note sheets were matched up with a notepad previously used by Patsy. No kidnapper would bring a notepad to write the ransom note inside the home. Nor could a kidnapper own a notepad with Patsy's writing already on it.

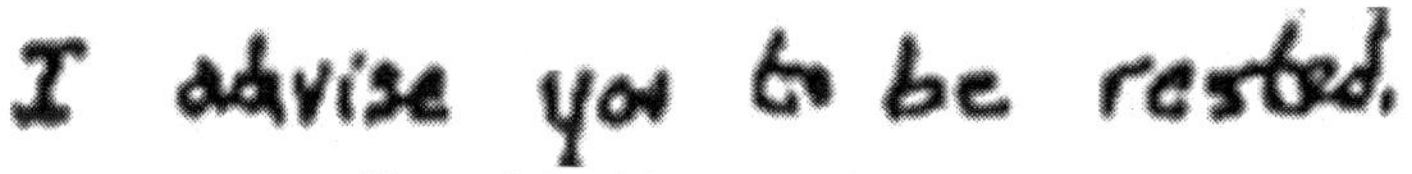

I advise you to be rested.

Figure 1: I advise you to be rested

Line 23 states, "I advise you to be rested". We need to place this within the context of the situation: according to the Ramseys, a kidnapper wrote the ransom note in the home while the parents are sleeping upstairs. Nobody advises sleeping parents to rest. This line in and by itself shows us the author of the note is not speaking from the perspective of actually going through the experience of a kidnapping. The author pretends to be outside the home with the kidnapped child. The author pretends to not be aware they are sleeping while we know the ransom note was written inside the home. It is by far more likely the author experienced fatigue by being up all night staging the scene and writing the letter. Remember, "we talk about that what is important to us first" and the line "I advise you to be rested" is a direct consequence of the writer's personal experience. His or her exhaustion triggered a sentence reflecting the author's reality. This sentence does not make sense within the context of the intruder theory.

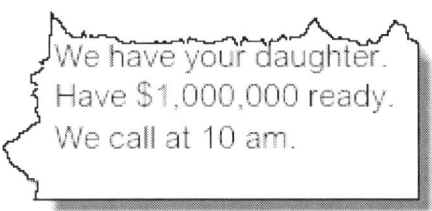

Figure 2: Sample typed ransom note

Kidnappers typically bring a short and typed note with them. Instead, the alleged kidnapper wrote a two-and-half page ransom note after the child's death. The foreign faction first explained where they are from and then left JonBenét's body behind in the Ramsey's basement. The kidnapper turned murderer introduced and identified himself. There is only one reason the note was written: it was part of staging, misdirection, and the first efforts to confuse investigators with the intent to throw them off. The writer had something macabre to hide in order to go through such an elaborate conspiracy process. The best questions to ask are: "what is the author hiding and why was this so important?"

The note is rambling at best. The author was filled with anxiety, longwinded, and confused. There is so much superfluous information and sidetracking away from the primary kidnapping message. The note has many inconsistencies and is far too long.

Characteristically, a storyline has three parts which are an introduction, event, and conclusion. The size percentages of each part are typically 25-50-25 percent. The ransom note is heavily skewed towards the event portion. The death threats in the middle portion are exaggerated to convince the readers.

	General	Ransom note
Introduction	25%	Line 1-11: 16%
Event	50%	Line 12-57: 72%
Conclusion	25%	Line 58-67: 12%

A typical ransom note is to the point with a dual focus: the ransom money and their leverage. Second, these notes are generally without an introduction and conclusion. Compare the directness of an average ransom note to the Ramsey ransom note:

Line 2-4 Introduction to who we are
Line 4-6 Compliments John Ramsey's business
Line 6-8 We have your daughter
Line 9-11 Threat
Line 12-13 Money demand
Line 15-21 Unusual instructions
Line 22-23 Advise to be rested
Line 23-28 Schedule flexibility on kidnapper's part
Line 29-65 Threats

Just like the 911 call, the child does not come first and is only the third priority. The number of words spent on threats is a whopping 59% of the total word count. Exaggeration is a tool to convince and suggests the threats are empty and hollow.

The introduction sentence, "We are a group of individuals that represent a small foreign faction" was likely written by someone under high-stress levels and not thinking with great clarity. A group refers to more than one person and an individual refers to one person. This suggests the group has no cohesion or, more likely, there was no group. No kidnapper would introduce, describe, and sign off with initials for investigators to have clues on how to find them. It is by far better to remain anonymous and not give any clue nor direction where to look for them. This is nonsense.

The use of a foreign faction is understandable since terrorism news items escalated in the 1990s. This was not very creative and a common scapegoat. Terrorism filled the news in abundance at the time and the media influence is clear. We are influenced by our environment.

Nobody refers to themselves as a small foreign faction. First, you are not foreign from your personal perspective. However, an outsider looking at a group may refer to the group as foreign. The author of the note is not part of the foreign faction rather an outsider looking in suggesting the group was fabricated. Second, you do not want to be seen as small when you need to be seen as powerful during a ransom situation. Third, a faction is an off-shoot of the small group which is now tiny.

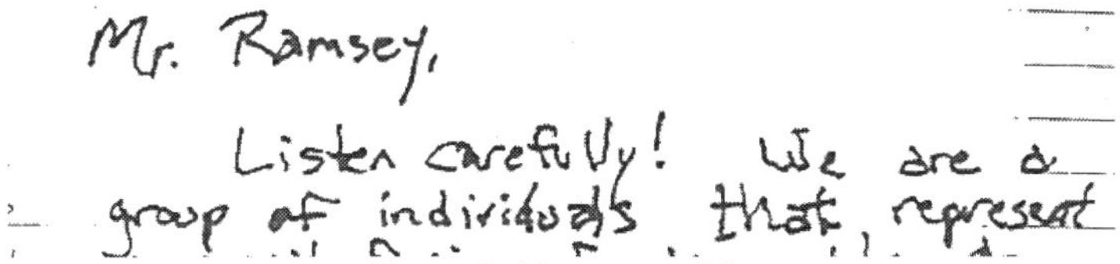

Figure 3: Listen carefully

The ransom note begins with "Mr. Ramsey, Listen carefully!" which means John specifically had to pay close attention to the message. The word "Listen" suggests he had to listen and implies the author probably talked with John prior to writing the note. The exclamation mark used for emphasis is like a demanding finger raised to keep someone's attention.

The words "Listen carefully" are mildly larger as compared to the writing that followed. This energy expansion implies the author made him or herself "big" and reflects on the demanding nature he or she portrayed. The exclamation mark emphasized the need to dominate and be forceful. The demanding nature implies the author wanted his undivided attention and means Mr. Ramsey needed to be convinced of something. The question is, "what did he need convincing of?"

The language use is sophisticated with words like attaché, adequate, hence, provoke, and deviation. The general word selection is in contrast with the misspelling of posession [sic] and bussiness [sic]. These mistakes seem to be deliberate and used to accentuate the idea the note was written by a non-English writer from a "foreign faction". However, the sophistication of the note tells us otherwise.

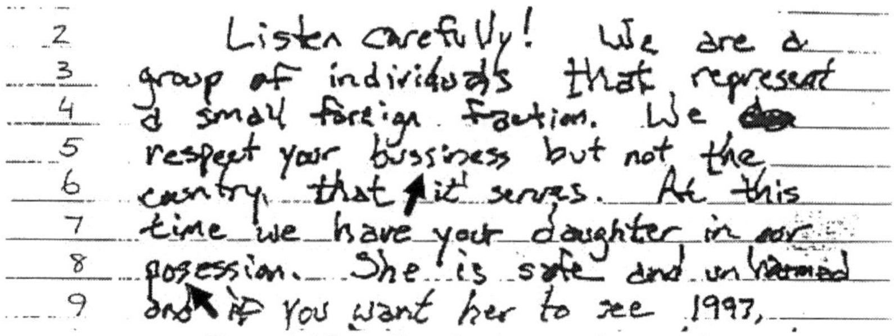

Figure 4: Misspellings business and possession

It is interesting to mention both misspellings happened at the beginning of the note and more specifically line 5 and 8. The beginning of any writing is where an author is still preoccupied with intrusive thoughts like "let me make spelling errors to make it look like a foreigner" to throw law enforcement off.

The second interesting observation is both spelling mistakes are identical using a change in the number of the letter /s and this supports the idea the errors were intentional. The first misspelling was creative while the second misspelling was an encounter with another word with /s and reminded the author to do it again.

There are phrases a foreigner would probably not use due to not understanding the significance. The line "use that Southern common sense" is personal and I doubt a foreigner would understand the implication of "Southern Pride" in the United States. The use of "law enforcement" is typical for Americans whereas outside the United States "police" is more prevalent.

There are a few acts of consideration in the note which do not make sense given the context of the kidnapping. The kidnappers are brutal enough to enter the home, intent to take a child and murder her. They are bold enough, in this case, to write the note in the home, and then leave the body behind. The circumstance and context simply do not match. The aggression of the alleged act and the caring attitude for the father of the victim are in direct contrast with each other.

15. Make sure that you bring an adequate size attache to the bank
Well, thank you, kidnapper. I would never have thought of that.

34. The gentlemen watching over your daughter
The word "Gentlemen" is not very scary when you attempt to intimidate the parents through fear in a kidnapping situation. The word selection "watching over" is also a curious one. Kidnappers watch your child as in monitor or keep an eye on. God watches over us and that may have been a Freudian slip very much like the word "gone" in the 911 call.

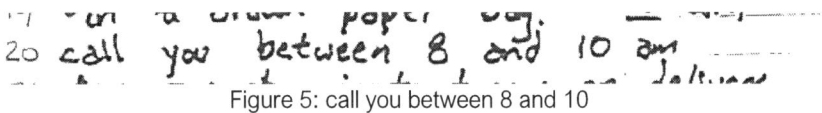
Figure 5: call you between 8 and 10

For a foreign faction as a team to scrutinize and monitor the Ramseys implies they are well organized. Yet, the best they can do is give a two-hour time frame to give instructions in a call for the delivery of the very thing they are after. Their money. These two perspectives contradict each other.

Two more examples showing the author did not live nor could imagine what a kidnapping would be like.

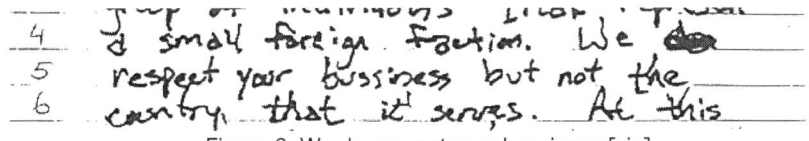
Figure 6: We do respect your bussiness [sic]

Line 5 states "We don't respect your bussiness [sic]". We can argue whether it says "don't" or "don" which is a distinction without a difference. The author changed perspective from "we do not" to "we do" respect. This is a crucial misstatement reflecting on not experiencing the kidnap circumstances.

The foreign faction made a compliment to the father of the child with, "We respect your bussiness [sic]" and made the compliment a priority over the kidnapping of his daughter. As innocent as the line, "We respect your bussiness [sic]" seems to be, it tells us the author is naïve and inexperienced about kidnapping scenarios. The full line reads, "we don respect your business but not the country it serves" which raises a question about victim selection. There is a shift from the individual Mr. Ramsey being addressed, to respect for his business, to the country he served. A foreign faction despising a country targets the epicenter of a country like the twin towers on September eleventh.

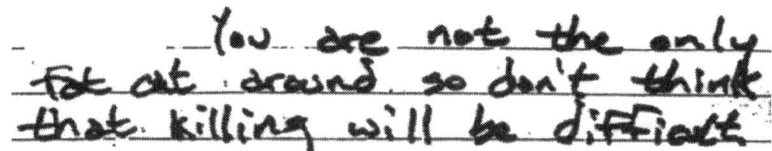
Figure 7: not the only fat cat

The author is fully aware he has a choice among millionaires as the "fat cat" line tells us. We would expect kidnapping for money would be easier when selecting someone you do not respect. The line, "but not the country it serves" shifts the focus to a political motivation. The foreign faction would have hurt the country more by kidnapping the child of a policymaker instilling fear in leadership.

From the perspective, "we talk about what is important to us first", respect for the father is prioritized over the kidnapping of his daughter used as leverage for financial gain. The fact Mr. Ramsey received a compliment first is in line with knowing him more intimately. A random intruder would not riddle the ransom note with niceties. The intimacy theme returned later in the note with "Mr. Ramsey" changing to "John" in the last paragraph. The author also knew John's ties to the south with the use of "Southern common sense".

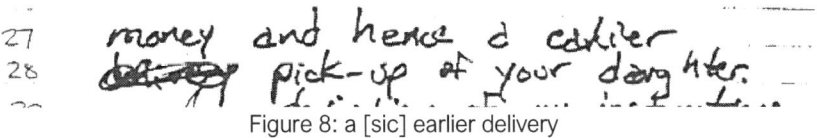
Figure 8: a [sic] earlier delivery

The change in perspective of earlier ~~delivery~~ to pick-up is another critical mistake showing the author did not experience the kidnapping but rather imagined what it would be like. A kidnapper would not increase the chance of being caught through a delivery. The correction shows the kidnapper's internal dialogue had two competing scenarios. In short, the kidnapping storyline is fabricated.

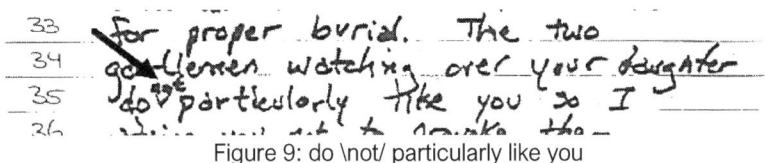
Figure 9: do \not/ particularly like you

The gentlemen do particularly like you was corrected to "do \not/ particularly like you". A change in perspective is a change in reality and a major red flag for deception. The author is an inept criminal and the storyline is demonstrably false.

The author also changed from a group perspective to singular and back to a group perspective. This substantial change, in reality, suggests again the pretends, fabricates, and went back and forth with different potential scenarios.

2. We are a group
7. our posession [sic]
10. our instructions
19. I will call you

25. We might call you
29. my instructions
53. our instructions

There is only one conclusion: there was no foreign faction and the storyline is fabricated.

Figure 10: Ransom "demand"

The ransom money amount is also odd. The sentence states, "you will withdraw $118,000 from your account". A kidnapper does not care where the money comes from. And this one apparently knew where the money was located: In Mr. Ramsey's account. Second, the ransom note does not demand a final and specific amount. The note says, "you will withdraw $118,000" but does not state whether this is the final amount or a first installment.

John Ramsey was worth six million in 1996. The ransom amount was rather small in comparison to his wealth. Line 59 reads, "You are not the only fat cat around" and tells us the alleged kidnappers are aware the Ramseys are wealthy. It makes no sense for this foreign faction to ask for just $118,000. We would expect thugs audacious enough to enter a home and take a child are bold enough to ask for big sums of money.

The ransom note is filled with discrepancies strongly suggesting the author is not an experienced criminal.

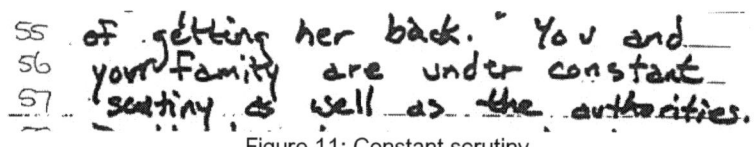
Figure 11: Constant scrutiny

The wording "constant scrutiny" implies every breath the Ramseys take is observed, recorded, and analyzed. This perspective does not match the two "if" statements.

23-24. if we monitor you getting the money earlier
40-41. if we catch you talking to a stray dog

The final chapter

A whole team scrutinizing and monitoring the Ramseys this close expects to catch them in an undesirable act and would use a "when" statement.

The ransom note has fourteen references to JonBenét and they are impersonal and distant. One would expect the kidnapper to pull on the heartstrings of the Ramseys by using her name to personalize and apply pressure to force them to comply.

7. your <u>daughter</u>
8. <u>She</u> is safe
9. if you want <u>her</u> to see 1997,
28. pickup of your <u>daughter</u>.
31. execution of your <u>daughter</u>
32. <u>her</u> remains
34. watching over your <u>daughter</u>

39. will result in your <u>daughter</u>
41. <u>she</u> dies.
42. <u>she</u> dies.
44. <u>she</u> dies
47. <u>she</u> dies.
52. your <u>daughter</u>
55. of getting <u>her</u> back.

We never veer far away from what we know, what we relate to, and return to what is familiar to us. Consider the word selection "execution" and "remains". The use of garrote is execution-style and "remains" refers to death. That is exactly what happened. There are no coincidences. Authors use words they relate to.

The impersonal references and emotional distance match the 911 call made by Patsy. She did not prioritize her daughter and did not create urgency to find the killer. And it matches John distancing himself in the CNN interview. He needed to know "why" it happened instead of "what" happened and distanced himself from solving the crime. With it, he negated the intruder theory and above all, distanced himself from his own daughter.

No intruder would kidnap a six-year-old girl for money, murder her, hide her in the basement, and take his time to write a two-and-a-half-page ransom note while leaving the leverage for the ransom behind. The note would have taken at least forty-five minutes if not an hour to write. The apparent lack of concern about being caught means the author of the note belonged in the home. Like a parent.

The intruder theory is utterly illogical, not probable, nor plausible, There was no physical evidence suggesting there was an intruder. The 911 call is deceptive and the ransom note was written by an inept criminal not experiencing an actual kidnapping. The author was unable to accurately gauge what a kidnapper would do.

There were only three survivors in the home. John, Patsy, and Burke. The sophistication of the note excludes the almost 10-year-old Burke as the author. So, who wrote the note: John or Patsy?

John was known to be stoic and calm under pressure. The likelihood he would write a rambling two-and-half-page ransom note is limited. It is also less likely he would write a ransom note addressing himself as "Mr. Ramsey" followed by "Listen carefully!" It is unlikely he would warn himself with "don't grow a brain, John". But someone looking at John could very well do that. "We respect your bussiness [sic]" is one of many clues Patsy is the author of the ransom note. And Patsy was known to do everything "Texas Style" which is in-line with the two-and-half pages.

The question is: Why was the note written in the first place?

In sum:
  a. The two-and-a-half-page ransom note is a farce
  b. The content of the note is rambling at best
  c. The ransom note was written in the home on a notepad belonging to Patsy Ramsey

Handwriting comparison analysis

The basis for Forensic Document Examination, or handwriting comparison analysis, is no two authors write the same. Lettering must follow formation standards to be recognizable for an /a to look like an /a. The foundation of letter formation is called class characteristics and people personalize their writing through a wide variety of options open to them. The combination of letter formation, handwriting movements, word spacing, slant, pressure, relative size, zonal distribution, arrangement on paper, etc. makes an author identifiable. An author will not write exactly the same twice due to changes in writing circumstances, differing moods, and natural variation. However, writing movements, spacing, etc. are highly habitual and tend to be fairly distinct and consistent.

In a mature writer, letter formations, stroke sequences, letter connections, etc. are habitual and ingrained. This is why we can differentiate one author from another. We discover unique and consistent patterns in writing behaviors like, but not limited to, speed, slant, spacing, placement on paper, pressure patterns, unique formations, connection strokes, diacritics, and punctuation, etc. Authors can be and often are, recognized by the existence of a unique combination of common traits and/or unique but uncommon traits. The likelihood of two different handwriting samples being one and the same author grows exponentially with the increase in characteristic handwriting similarities.

Handwriting comparison analysis is an elaborate process that finds consistencies in known handwriting exemplars which are compared to questioned samples. Multiple people involved in the JonBenét Ramsey case provided handwriting samples including John and Patsy Ramsey.

The consensus among various independent handwriting experts is that Patsy Ramsey is the author of the ransom note.

1. Gideon Epstein - Forensic Document Examiner: "Based on the presently available documents, there are strong indications that Patsy Ramsey is the author of the ransom note."

2. David S. Liebman - Certified Document Examiner: "There are far too many similarities and consistencies revealed in the handwriting of Patsy Ramsey and the ransom note for it to be coincidence. In light of the number of comparisons and similarities between Patsy Ramsey and the ransom note writer the chances of a third party also sharing the same characteristics is astronomical. In my professional opinion, Patsy Ramsey is the ransom note writer."

3. Tom Miller - Attorney, Court Qualified Expert Witness in Questioned Documents: "Based upon available exemplars compared to the purported "ransom" note in the JonBenét Ramsey murder, the handwriting is probably that of Patsy Ramsey."

4. Chet Ubowski - Colorado Bureau of Investigation Handwriting Expert: "This handwriting showed indications that the writer was Patsy Ramsey." He said to have found 24 of 26 letters[5] in the ransom note which matched exemplars from Patsy Ramsey. In private, Mr. Ubowski stated, "Patsy wrote the note".

5. Cina L. Wong - Certified Document Examiner: "I have made careful examination and comparison of the 'ransom' note and the exemplars of Patsy Ramsey. I have reached the conclusion that the handwritings and 'ransom' note were very probably written by the same person...it is my professional opinion that Patsy Ramsey

---

[5] Chet Ubowski took a conservative stance being part of the Boulder political scene. But 24 of 26 similarities in letter formations it is a foregone conclusion Patsy is the author.

very likely wrote the 'ransom' note. In a YouTube presentation, she claimed to have noticed over 200 similarities (Wong 2016).

6. Larry F. Ziegler - Forensic Document Examiner: "It was determined and is still determined by myself that Patsy Ramsey is the writer of the ransom note."

7. Marcel Elfers – Questioned Document Examiner: "The ransom note author and Patsy Ramsey are highly likely the same author".

There is a consensus Patsy wrote the note and I agree as a Questioned Document Examiner with their assessments. Of course, Team Ramsey found their experts and they dispute the findings of these seven independent document examiners.

Handwriting comparison samples

The following section provides a mere glance at what Questioned Document Examiners look for. The samples are labeled (1) for known Patsy handwriting. The samples labeled (2) are the author of the ransom note. The most common similarities have been documented already with an emphasis on letter construction. The following samples are some similarities in arrangement, letters, and letter combinations.

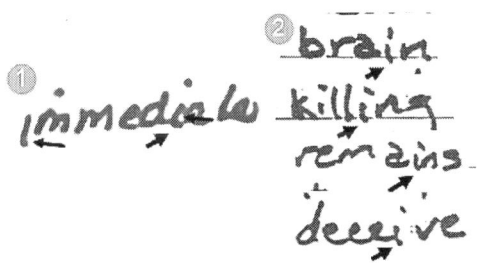

Figure 12: Immediate vs brain killing remains deceive

The Mid-Zone-i's have distinct similarities. The Mid-Zone-i drops below the baseline and bends a tad forward at the bottom. These writing movements are subconscious and authors are not aware they do this. This characteristic is habitual in the ransom note and Patsy has the same feature in her known writing.

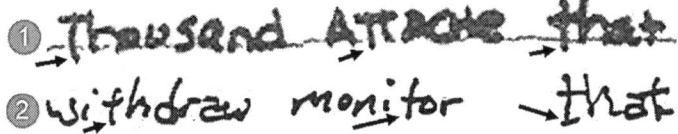

Figure 13: Letter /t drops below the baseline

The letter /t also moves through the baseline as the /i's do. The /t bend forward on the bottom is also present. This similarity in the /i and the /t support each other as a habitual characteristic present in Patsy's writing and the author of the ransom note.

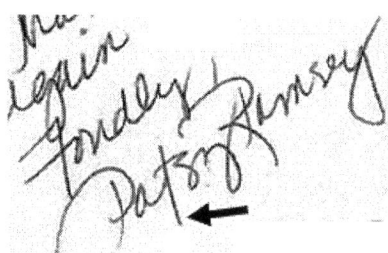

Figure 14: Patsy Ramsey drops t below the baseline

Patsy's cursive writing decisively moves the /t through the baseline in her signature. The height of the letter /t incidentally refers to the degree of pride in accomplishments. Very tall /t stems imply a stronger need for accomplishing things and goes hand-in-hand with perseverance, not acknowledging limitations, and excessiveness. This characteristic is in line with a two-and-a-half-page ransom note.

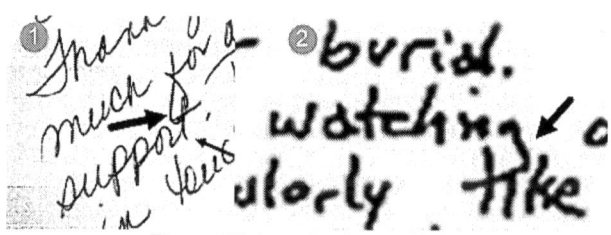

Figure 15: Invasive Lower Zone

The Lower Zone structures going through the next line is called an Invasive Lower Zone[6]. In actuality, the next line moves through the previous Lower Zone structure. Patsy and the ransom note author match. Kimon Iannetta explains this feature is linked to confusion of interests, spreading oneself thin, and subjective thinking. This writing characteristic supports the /i and /t going through the baseline. Such writers overdo things and tend to be gluttonous.

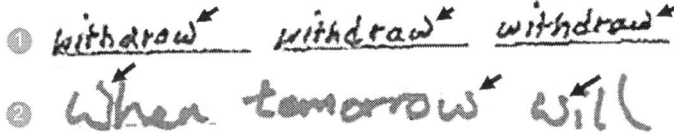

Figure 16: Withdraw final w pull up and to left

The ransom note author (2) and Patsy (1) tend to pull the final Up Stroke (↑) of the /w up and to the left.

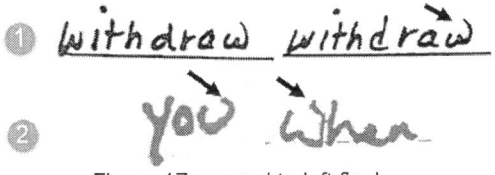

Figure 17: up and to left finals

The finals of Up Strokes (↑) are prone to end up and to the left in the /u as well.

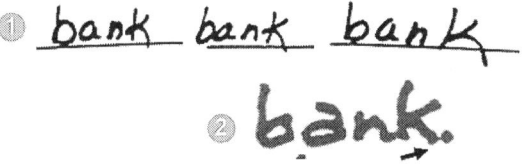

Figure 18: banK

Both the ransom note author (2) and Patsy (1) enlarge the /k. The personality trait attached to this feature is "defiance-to-authority".

---

[6] Kimon Iannetta, author of "Danger Between The Lines"

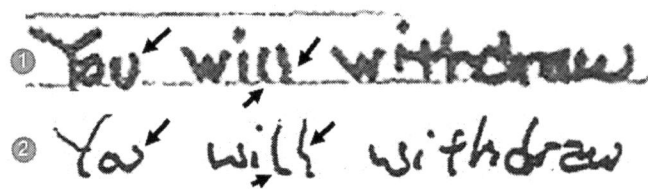

Figure 19: You will withdraw

The requested writing of Patsy (1) has a stunning similarity with the ransom note sentence (2). The now calmer Patsy (1) has a similar movement with less amplitude in the /u and /l as compared to the ransom note. This suggests Patsy went through the same emotional experience when writing the requested writing (1).

Figure 20: Country similarities

Patsy and the ransom note author have similar /t to /r connections. It is extremely hard if not impossible to mimic or forge the combination of the higher /c extending above the /u with the /o decreasing in size.

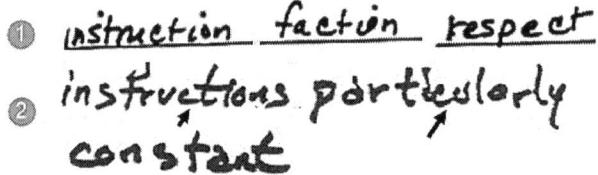

Figure 21: /c extension

A distinct habitual tendency in Patsy's known writing (1) is the unusual extension of the final of the letter /c. The ransom note author (2) owns the same characteristic.

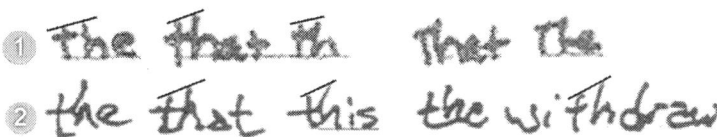

Figure 22: /th combination

Patsy (1) and the ransom note author (2) share a successive higher stroke in the /th combination. The stem of the /h is habitually higher than the /t.

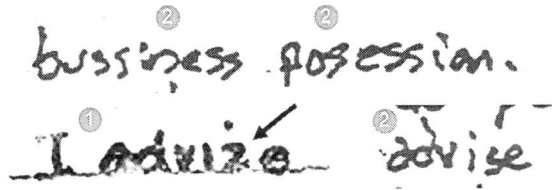

Figure 23: I advize [sic]

The misspelling of the common words is a mind-blowing similarity in behavior and perspective. The ransom note author misspelled bussiness [sic] and posession [sic]. The latter word was likely triggered by the encounter of the double /s. Patsy wrote the requested writing sample labeled (1). Lo and behold, Patsy spelled "advize [sic]" with a /z. The /s in the word "advise" once again prompted Patsy to misspell. We can safely assume the mistake is willful and deliberate. Patsy was an intelligent woman with a degree in journalism.

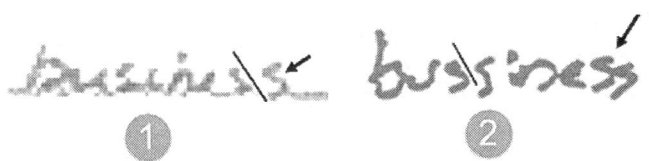

Figure 24: /s similarities

The similarities in the letter /s are striking. The /s bottom is heavier, protrudes mildly forward, and some /s's slant backward.

Similarities are not limited to letter formations, connection strokes, size sequences, etc. We see similarities in punctuation as well.

Figure 25: Mr. floating period

The London test letter is a fictitious text and includes all letters and numbers. The text is used for comparison purposes.

There are three prominent similarities in "Mr." Patsy's writing in the London test letter (1) and the ransom note (2) are a match.
The /M starts with a Down Stroke (↓), the mid-stem does not come down the baseline, and the period is floating mid /r.

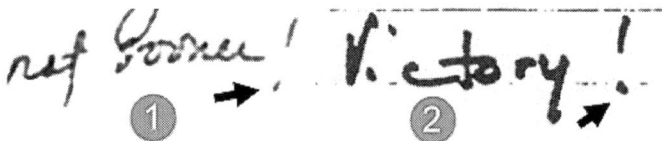

Figure 26: Exclamation period drops below baseline

Patsy dropped the exclamation mark period below the baseline in her known writing (1). And although this is less pronounced in the ransom note, the period has dropped. The same handwriting characteristic often occurs in varying degrees and is referred to as natural variation.

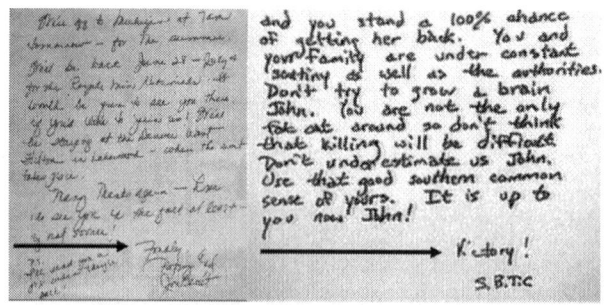

Figure 27: Signage placement to the right

The final chapter

Patsy signing letters to the right is a similarity in placement. This characteristic supports the letters /i, /t, exclamation mark, and the invasive Lower Zone. Down Strokes (↓) and moving forward are action-oriented.

Questioned document examiners compare known writings with questioned writings and look for similarities and dissimilarities in habitual tendencies. The more habitual similarities are present, the more likely the known and questioned authors are one and the same. This is a reasonable conclusion.

The samples shown above are listed below. The samples are limited and there are many more habitual similarities.

1. Mid-Zone-i drops below baseline.
2. Mid-Zone-i bends forward at the bottom.
3. /t drops below the baseline.
4. /t bends forward at the bottom.
5. Invasive Lower Zone.
6. /w and /u last stem bend to up and left.
7. Enlarged /k buckle.
8. Final /k drops below baseline.
9. Letter combination /cou is similar in height sequence.
10. The /c has a lengthened bottom horizontal.
11. The /th combination shows a taller /h stem.
12. The /s has a smaller and more withdrawn top.
13. The /M retraced the first stem.
14. The /M mid-stem does not come down to the bottom.
15. The period in Mr. floats.
16. The period of exclamation mark drops below baseline.
17. The signage placement is on the right.

The ransom note author and Patsy own many similar handwriting characteristics. In my opinion, Patsy is the author of the ransom note beyond a reasonable doubt. There is a mathematical equation to explain the certitude of an opinion based on chance.

Steve Thomas

On April 10, 2000, Elizabeth Vargas interviewed Detective Steve Thomas on "Good morning America":

Vargas: "Thomas says investigators interviewed 590 people, investigated and cleared more than 100 suspects, and collected 1,058 pieces of evidence. But the trail always led back to one place. That epic ransom note. The note asked for $118,000 and claimed to be from a small foreign faction and was signed by the mysterious S.B.T.C. Three pages of crucial clues. Thomas says they checked handwriting samples from 73 potential suspects, but only one person could not be ruled out as the author."
Thomas: "And that one person happens to be Patsy Ramsey".

Thomas explained Patsy's penchant for the use of acronyms returned in the ransom note. And Patsy used the lower-case manuscript /a in her pre-homicide writings and in the note. She changed her /a's to lower cursive /a's after she was made aware of this similarity. He further mentioned other likenesses like indentation and the use of exclamation marks.

Glove

Laurence Smith stated in his book Patsy wore a glove to disguise her handwriting. And I quote, "… a person can easily disguise their handwriting by wearing a glove on their writing hand that serves to convert their handwriting to being virtually unrecognizable".

This statement is only partially true and not applicable in the JonBenét ransom note case for a very good reason. Although Patsy may have worn a glove, it did not affect her handwriting sufficiently to disguise it.

Handwriting is a behavior requiring control of fine motor skills in the hand musculature guided by visual feedback. It stands to reason a thin latex glove does not reduce the quality of handwriting. A thick foam-lined welding glove would decrease control over pen grip, fine motor skills, and hinder visual feedback. The writing tends to remain similar in habitual movements and loss of control over details.

The ransom note author controlled fine motor skills to a large extent as seen in the details of the handwriting.

Patsy requested writing

Ransom note author

Figure 28: glove did not alter detail

The multitude of similarities in the details has shown us sufficient evidence to conclude Patsy is the author. A potential glove did not alter her handwriting beyond recognition.

Mathematical probability

The premise of handwriting comparison analysis is no two people write the same. All writers will personalize their handwriting making an author identifiable. Handwriting is highly habitual and there are many factors to consider including, but not limited, to letter formation, connection strokes, line-word-letter spacing, use of punctuation, slant, relative size capitals to name a few.

In handwriting comparison analysis, it is imperative to find consistent and unique patterns whatever they may be. Writers are unaware of their subconscious habits. The more habitual patterns are present, the more likely two authors are one and the same.

We may be able to quantify the likelihood with a chance model like the coin toss. One flip of a coin gives us a 50% chance. It is either heads (H) or tails (T). The chance we guess the sequence correctly with two tosses is harder because there are four possible outcomes. We can guess HH, HT, TH, and T. This is a one in four or 25% chance.

		chance
1 toss	½	1:2
2 tosses	½ x ½	1:4
3 tosses	½ x ½ x ½	1:8
4 tosses	½ ^4	1:16
5 tosses	½ ^5	1:32
10 tosses	½^10	1:1,024
20 tosses	½^20	1:1,048,576

The table shows our chance to guess the sequence correctly with five flips of a coin is 1 in 32. At twenty tosses, we have a one in one million-plus chance. Nobody in their right mind would take these odds.

This principle can be applied to handwriting comparison analysis with a twist. Individual letters can be written differently. There is a wide variety in how we can form, size, and space letters. Take the /r for instance:

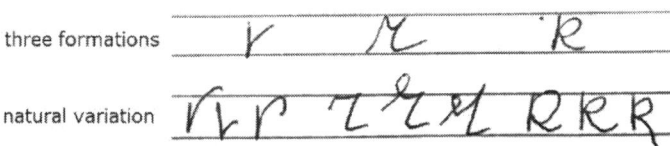

three formations

natural variation

Figure 29: three /r's with natural variation

There are at minimum three different /r formations as shown in the sample. Each letter will have natural variation within the basic structure. It is a safe assumption that letters can be written in at least four different ways on average. The chance two writers have one similar letter formation is, therefore, a one in four chance. In other words, on average, we only need four authors to find a writer who has one similar letter with a known writer. The probability two authors have one letter formation similarity is very high. It would take sixteen samples to find two similarities and one-thousand-twenty-four to find five similarities.

Letter formation	4 letter formations	chance
1 similarity	1/4	1:4
2 similarities	1/4^2	1:16
5 similarities	1/4^5	1:1,024
10 similarities	1/4^10	1:1,048,576
15 similarities	1/4^15	1:1,073,741,824
24 similarities	1/4^24	1: 281 trillion[+]

The odds two authors are one and the same increases dramatically with more similarities. Chet Ubowski, the handwriting expert for the Boulder Police Department, found 24 of 26 similarities in letter formations. The chance an intruder would have the same number of similarities is 1: 281 trillion-plus. Even if we cut his findings in half, the odds a random intruder had the same twelve similarities in letter formations as one of the inhabitants in the house is 1 in 16,777,216. These odds equal the accuracy of DNA analysis. Investigators and handwriting experts determined Patsy Ramsey is highly likely to author of the ransom note. The chance a random intruder had these similarities with Patsy's writing is astronomically small. Yours truly opines Patsy is the author of the note proven beyond a reasonable doubt.

Handwriting analysis

Handwriting analysts look at handwriting behaviors and the symbolism behind them. Handwriting analysis or graphology is different from handwriting comparison analysis. A graphologist attaches a personality trait value to writing.

A good analogy to explain the difference between handwriting analysis and handwriting comparison analysis is observing someone crossing his arms. The comparison analysis observes the right arm is over the left. The graphologist attaches a value like a defensive posture or he is cold. This chapter is about matching handwriting behaviors with personality traits.

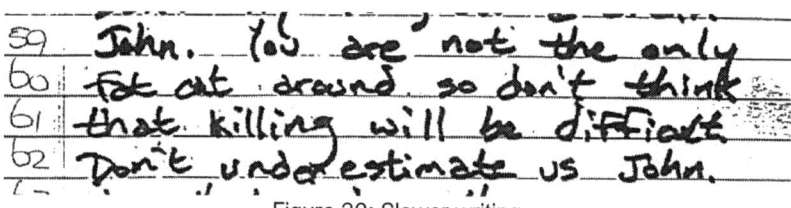

Figure 30: Slower writing

The overall slower and disconnected writing with wider spacing shows the author was cautious, took the time to think about what to say and how to say it. The writer was anxious, emotional, and guarded. This implies pretense and hiding behind a façade. The writer was consciously aware of planning, correcting, and had a goal in mind. Within the context of the note, the goal was deceit and misdirection.

The general consistency in letter formation, precise punctuation in the Mid-Zone-i's, and the corrections made show the author is meticulous and crafts a message rather than a spontaneous expression. Spontaneous writing is a means to express whereas carefully crafting is to impress or convince.

Up Strokes (↑) move symbolically towards imagination, the spiritual, reasoning, morality, etc. Up Strokes (↑) need to come back to the Mid Zone or the reality zone.

Figure 31: Letter d stem ends upward

This author writes many /d's in an unusual way. The body of the /d is formed counter-clockwise and the stem is formed with an Up Stroke (↑) and then does not come back down. We see in the far-right sample the /d stem was made with an Up Stroke (↑) while the Down Stroke (↓) was initiated but not finalized.

The symbolism in handwriting analysis suggests the writer stays in the imagination zone and symbolically represents a thought not matched with reality.

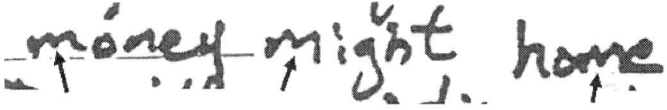

Figure 32: Letter /m mid-stem does not come down

The same principle, not coming down towards the reality baseline, is seen in the mid-stem of the letter /m. Down Strokes (↓) are action-oriented strokes. Limiting, withholding, and falling short of this action shows insecurity regarding a thought process or the truthfulness of an insight. Authors, who habitually do not come down to the baseline, may lose or have lost touch with reality. Symbolically speaking, the imagination zone is not being connected with the reality zone.

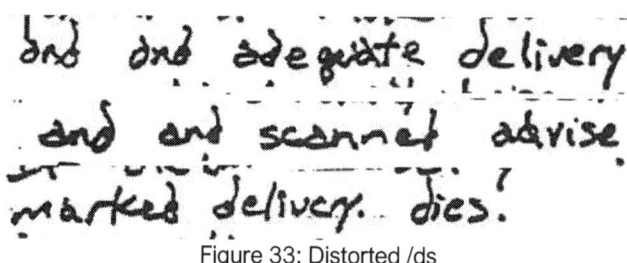
Figure 33: Distorted /ds

The Up Strokes (↑) are movements toward the imagination zone. A writer who is secure within themselves and confident in their thoughts, ideas, and moral standards, will write Up Strokes (↑) firmly. The strokes are fluid, straight, and smooth.

The letter /d represents our personal value system. This may include ideas, morals, beliefs, appearance, or general lifestyle (Iannetta 2008)[7]. The letter /d starts in the reality zone, moves upward into the imagination zone, and needs to come down to reality once again. Symbolically speaking, the letter starts in reality, is evaluated during a thought process, and should come back to reality to be checked for veracity.

Distortions in the letter /d imply an author is anxious about their value system and whether it is accepted by their environment. The more significant the distortions, the more they feel their value system is rejected, and the more insecure the author is. The author of the ransom note has severely distorted letter /d's as compared to other Upper Zone structures.

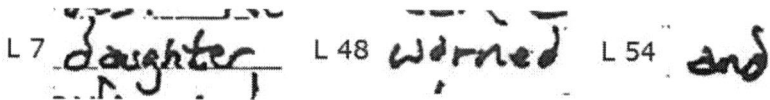
Figure 34: Letter /d stem does not improve over time

The letter /d does not improve over time as the /t does. The continued distortions in the letter /d imply the author feared

---

[7] Page 178

rejection over moral standards within the context of the events that night. The author knew what happened was unacceptable.

Figure 35: scrutiny is cramped up

The word "scrutiny" is cramped up and distorted. This is in line with the distortions of the letter /d. The author felt their morality would be questioned and the thought of constant scrutiny created angst, pain, and fear forcing the letters to cramp up.

Figure 36: k buckle enlarged

An enlarged /k buckle relative to other Mid Zone structures implies the author, at least at the time of the writing, was defiant and rebellious. Defiance is particularly linked to the /k but can be seen in other oversized Mid Zone letters as well.

Disguise

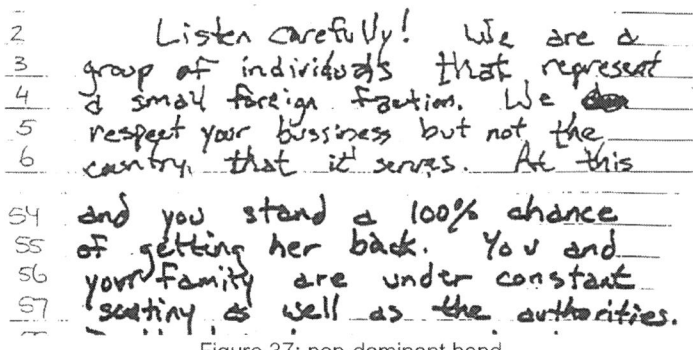
Figure 37: non-dominant hand

The ransom note was likely written with the non-dominant hand in the belief the handwriting could be disguised. The first paragraph has by far less control as compared to the last paragraph.

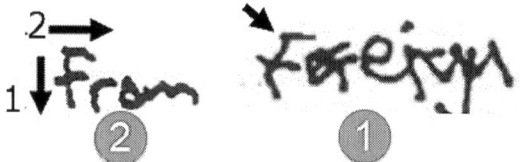

Figure 38: /F two strokes

The idea the non-dominant hand was used is supported by the two-stroke formation of the /f. For a right-handed individual like Patsy, the left would have been used. The /f is formed in two strokes in the ransom note (2) and suggests the author was not used to making a one-stroke /f. The two-stroke formation returned in the requested writing of Patsy in the /f of "foreign" (1).

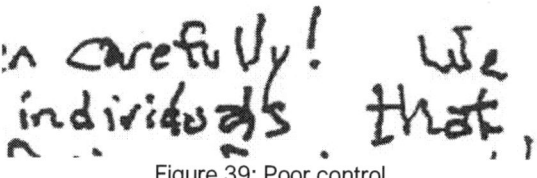

Figure 39: Poor control

Poor control is seen in many aspects of this handwriting. There are striking variations in letter size, letter spacing, and slant. Note also how many of the Down Strokes (↓) are wiggled which implies the author was unsure about what to do. Firm straight Down Strokes (↓) belong to a strong and decisive writer. Such writers have "a spine" so to say. This writer is the opposite. Unsure and shaken to the core is emphasized by a non-dominant hand.

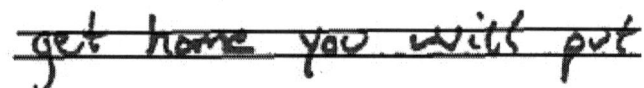

Figure 40: Mid Zone structures

The Mid Zone is the area where letters like /a, /c, /m, etc. reside and the bodies of the /b and body of the /g. the Mid Zone is our here-and-now and our reality zone. This zone shows our confidence levels within social settings and whether we feel accepted or not. Good quality writing in the Mid Zone shows rhythmic, consistent, and harmonious writing.

The ransom note writer is inconsistent in lcttcr formation, spacing, and slant to name a few. This suggests the writer had a problem with anxiety at the time of writing. Anxiety happens when you do not know where you stand on issues and have a hard time dealing with reality, current events, and confusion. The distorted letter formations suggest poor thinking patterns, confusion, and unrealistic thought patterns.

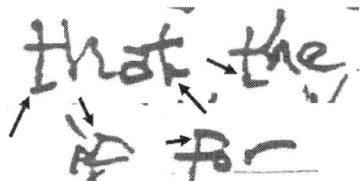

Figure 41: /t bottom and /f top added

The author formed the /t with just a stem Down Stroke (↓) and then added the bottom crossbar. The level of intelligence of this author is relatively high. Looking at word selection and sentence construction implies the author's handwriting is expected to be fluid like the second part of the note. These corrections enforce the idea the author wrote with the non-dominant hand in an effort to disguise.

The writing became more natural and smoother as the note moved on. The difference between the first paragraph and the last is enormous. The non-dominant hand may have gone through a learning curve and developed the writing skills. Another plausible reason is she switched back to her dominant hand because it was too cumbersome, tiresome, or took too much time.

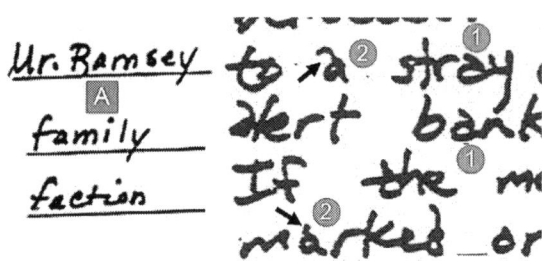

Figure 42: Corrections to the /a

The letter /a is of particular interest. Patsy changed her /a to differ from the ransom note /a (2). Suddenly Patsy changed to the script /a. We see how several /*a*'s received the top tail as an add-on (2) to make it look like an /a and different from /*a*. This furthers the idea the writing was deliberately disguised. Now ask yourself: What random intruder needs to disguise their handwriting with the offender assuming he will never be caught?

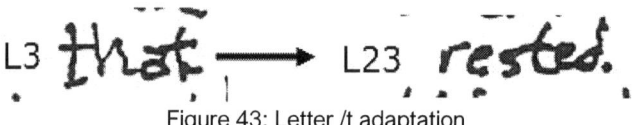

Figure 43: Letter /t adaptation

The author adapted well and started to automate the change in the letter /t from a straight down /t stem to one with a forward-moving crossbar on the bottom by line 23.

Handwriting comparison analysis points to Patsy as the author who attempted to disguise her writing and tried to make it look a foreigner wrote the ransom note. It makes perfect sense for Patsy to disguise herself as a known entity in the home.

Patsy's behavior

An all too brief introduction to behavioral trend analysis. One of the best personality models, and gaining popularity, is the Enneagram.

The Enneagram is a systematic, dynamic, and progressive personality model mapping behavioral trends and the motivation behind them. The Enneagram is based on psychological principles and explains our lens of perspective forms in the first three to five years. A child is motivated to compensate to be appreciated and to belong. We own go-to-emotions, go-to-thoughts, and go-to-behaviors as a distinct pattern. Personality is defined as a set of habitual tendencies. Motivation, combined with behavioral trends, forms our "Priority Theme".

"Our view of the world is a childhood view carried forward"

We fall back on what we are most familiar with especially when stressed. We are hard-wired to return toward the familiar and move away from the unfamiliar. And the Ramsey situation was enormously stressful.

The Enneagram tells us there are nine types all owning a distinct Priority Theme. This theme consists of a core belief system, attitude, and habitual compensatory behaviors. Don Riso and Russ Hudson (D. R. Riso 1996) made the most substantial contribution mapping each of the nine Types' core fears and their compensatory behaviors. Their "Levels of Development" is a progressive overview of behavioral style, motivation, and predictability.

Type Two[8]
We are born with natural abilities and are influenced by our environment. A Type Two child grew up feeling loved and appreciated only when they were good to others first. They become helpers and people pleasers. This early childhood perspective old them to prioritize others' needs before their own. These children, and later as adults, see themselves as loving,

---

[8] See: "One Reason; an overview of likeability"

caring, giving, and sacrificial. They tend to volunteer to assist and may spread themselves thin. Their innate need to be good to others means they must socialize and befriend others so they can be good to them.

Their speaking style reflects their core attitude as they tend to sympathize, comfort, pitch in, engage, assist, and advise. Simply stated, type Twos love to be needed. This fits Patsy's known behaviors who volunteered for many functions and was socially active in the Boulder community.

From all accounts, Patsy was a loving and caring mother who lived vicariously through her daughter. She was a beauty queen herself and did everything Texas-style including JonBenét's make-up, hair, and outfits. She loved to entertain, was generous, loved people, and needed them. A healthy Type Two is altruistic, empathetic, and wants the best for others. On average, they are filled with good intentions. All too often, the needs of others outweigh personal needs. They may become intrusive by making themselves needed and provide unwanted advice and assistance. Their strong emotions drive them into immediate action.

Type Twos process information primarily emotionally and when stressed, they act out their emotions and become highly reactive. However, at stressful times, abstract reasoning goes by the wayside as emotions overwhelm them. They become domineering, highly reactive, and irrational. With this in mind, the mix of a caring and yet dominant attitude in the ransom note makes sense.

Don Foster, an esteemed linguistics professor, said it best. "We cannot falsify who we are. Sentence structure, word usage, and identifying features can be a signature." I cannot agree more as a Questioned Document Examiner. There are definitely many consistencies with Patsy's wording, sentence construction, use of acronyms, spelling habits, indentations, grammar, word selection, spacing, and use of acronyms. Foster's opinion was loud and clear: "In my opinion, it is not possible that any individual except Patsy Ramsey wrote the ransom note".

The ransom note started with dominance. The stressed-out Patsy took charge on the first page:
Line 2. <u>Listen</u> carefully!
Line 10. You <u>must</u> follow
Line 12. You <u>will</u> withdraw
Line 15. <u>Make</u> sure
Line 18. You <u>will</u> put the money

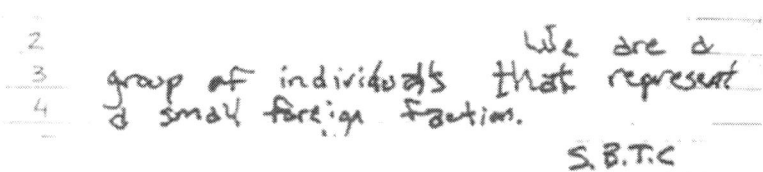
Figure 44: Introduction and signage

The ransom note was addressed to Mr. Ramsey. Patsy, the would-be-kidnapper, could not resist being socially appropriate. The foreign faction introduced themselves and signed with S.B.T.C [no period]. An introduction gives investigators tools to work with and tells them where to look and search for the name linked to S.B.T.C [no period]. This does not make sense from the kidnapper's perspective. It makes perfect sense for Patsy with her innate need to be kind and caring. The sentence construction, "we are a group of individuals" is odd and suggests high levels of anxiety.

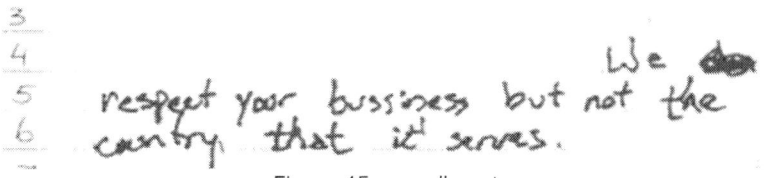
Figure 45: compliments

The social niceties continued in line 5. John received a compliment stating, "We respect for your bussiness [sic]". Kidnappers taking a child and complimenting the father is a contradiction of respect versus disrespect and suggests fabrication.

Patsy could not help but provide unwanted advice with, "Make sure that you bring an adequate size attache to the bank" and, "The delivery will be exhausting so I advise you to be rested".

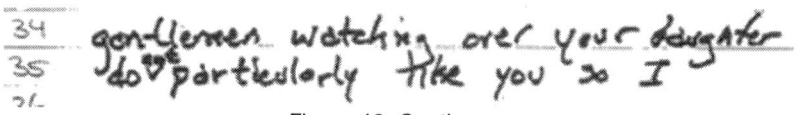
Figure 46: Gentlemen

Patsy, in her dire need to be appropriate, referred to hardcore criminals who just killed her daughter as "gentlemen".

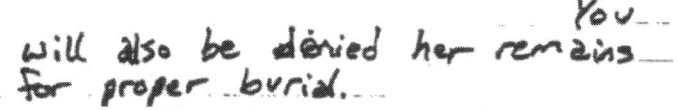
Figure 47: denial of a proper burial

The alleged kidnapper shows with "proper burial" awareness of appropriate social standards. This would be of no concern to kidnappers but makes sense from Patsy's good intentions perspective. Unwittingly, Patsy provided clues for investigators about who wrote the note.

Type Two, who sees wrong being done, can become explosively violent, domineering, and even ruthless. They are highly reactive because abhorrent behaviors go straight against their grain of "always being good".

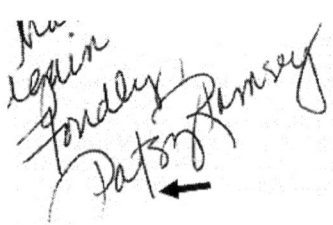
Figure 48: Patsy letter /t

82

Handwriting characteristics will be addressed in the next chapter. The /t barreling through the baseline implies an ability to overdo things and overstep boundaries.

In sum:
The empathy mixed with the domineering stress reaction matches Patsy's known behaviors as an Enneagram Type Two.

Emotional impact

Handwriting analysis is not just about observing writing movements and attaching symbolic meaning. Recognizing emotional influences can be seen in handwriting and may provide other important clues within the context of what has been written.

People who are excited, elated, and filled with enthusiasm tend to make themselves bigger. The principle of expansion returns in handwriting and is an expression of energy levels.

Figure 49: I love you

The "I love you" author meant what she wrote. The rise in "you" shows an increase in energy as the pen reached higher and higher. The "what" and "how" it is written match.

People who feel sadness, sorrow, pain, and anguish slump their shoulders and hang their heads down. Their energy levels decreased as they fight negative emotions. Their handwriting tends to become more compact and baselines tend to drop.

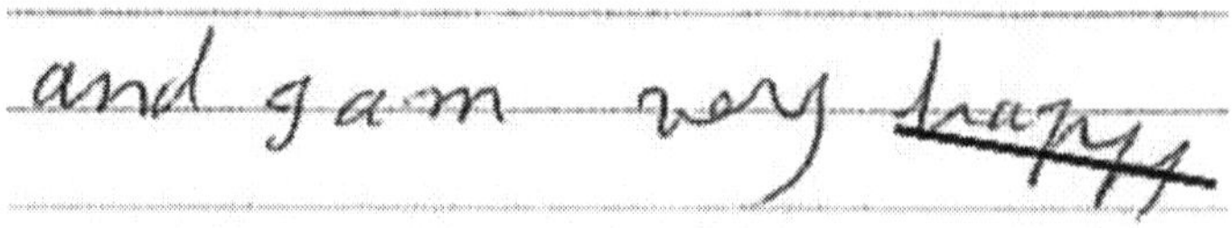

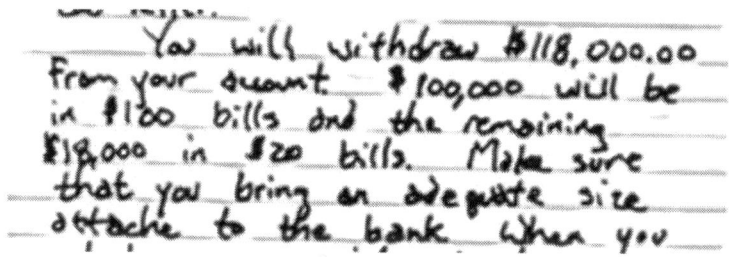

Figure 50: I am very happy

The "I am very happy" sample author wrote she is happy. The Personal Pronoun I and the /v drop below the baseline, and the word "happy" slants down. This is significant because the author cramped up and lost her drive to reach higher to stay on the provided guideline. The sentence and the writing behavior conflict with each other.

There are also significant indicators showing the author knew the child was seriously harmed or dead at the time of the writing. The ransom note has important emotional reactions to its content.

Figure 51: page one on the line

Patsy stayed on the line on page one and was consistently below the baseline on page two. Page two contains the death language where she talked about JonBenét's being beheaded and dying.

pick-up of your daughter.
Any deviation of my instructions
will result in the immediate
execution of your daughter. You
will also be denied her remains
for proper burial. The two
gentlemen watching over your daughter
do not particularly like you so I
advise you not to provoke them.
Speaking to anyone about your
situation, such as Police, F.B.I., etc.,
will result in your daughter being
beheaded. If we catch you talking
to a stray dog, she dies. If you
alert bank authorities, she dies.
If the money is in any way
marked or tampered with, she
dies. You will be scanned for
electronic devices and if any are

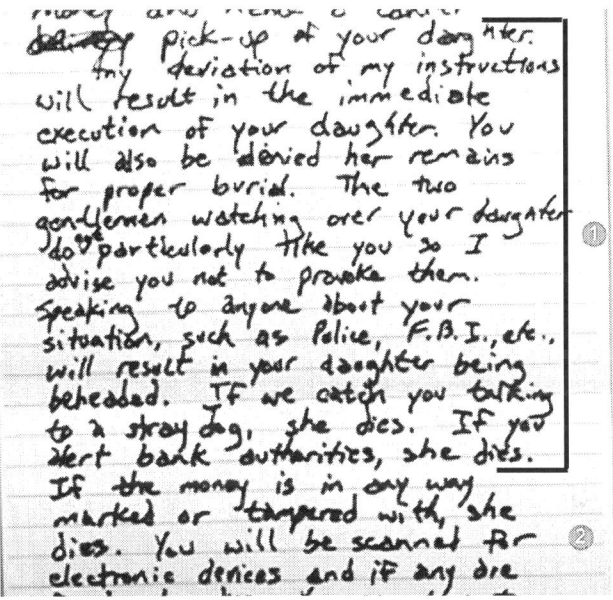

Figure 52: page two below the line

This is noteworthy from an emotional impact perspective. She was distracted by the thoughts of death, knew she was in the basement, and cramped up. In section (2) where the abstract subject money starts, she returns to write on the baseline including on page three.

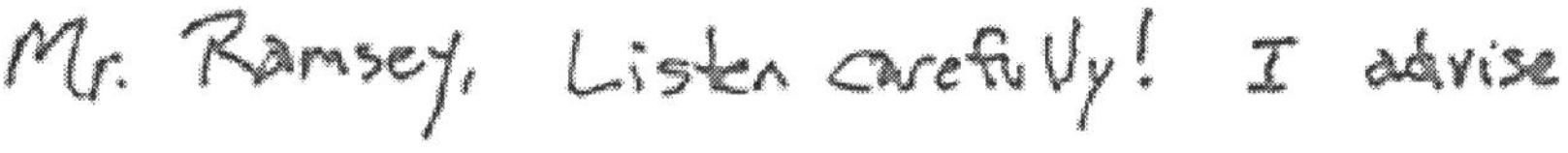

Mr. Ramsey, Listen carefully! I advise

Figure 53: Capital size

The size of capitals, and especially the Personal Pronoun I, reveal our self-esteem. The capitals in the ransom note are a good size and suggest a confident author.

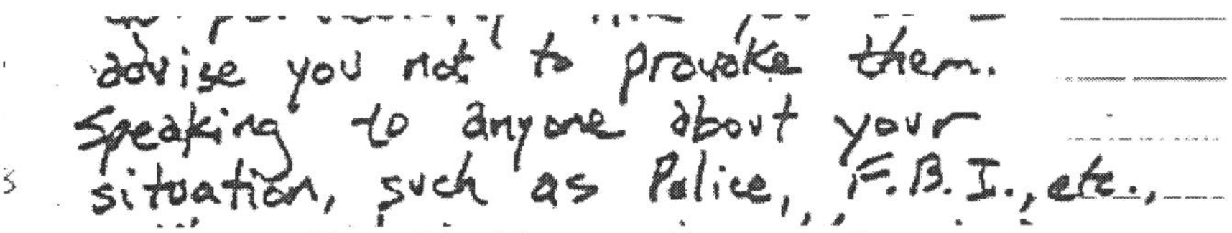

advise you not to provoke them.
Speaking to anyone about your
situation, such as Police, F.B.I., etc.,

Figure 54: advise you not to provoke them

The Mid-Zone-i size symbolically represents our confidence levels in social settings and the size suggests the author is comfortable. Patsy was a known socialite and a social butterfly.

An author may reveal their emotional state through size changes. A writer who becomes anxious may cramp up their writing. Lettering may become smaller, closer together, and/or distort their habitual stroke pattern. One of the first things I noticed seeing the ransom note for the first time was the sentence "She is safe and unharmed". It was instantly clear; the author was emotionally affected by the word "unharmed".

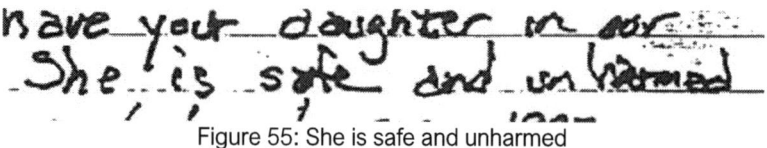
Figure 55: She is safe and unharmed

The sentence, she is safe and unharmed" has two very significant clues that may go unnoticed to an inexperienced eye.

On a side note, Patsy said in the CNN interview, "JonBenét is safe and with God". People never veer far away from what they know including their speech pattern and word selection. We cannot help but take note of the similarities.

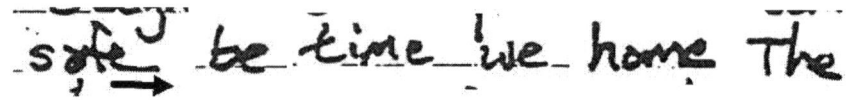
Figure 56: longer final /e

The word "safe" owns an extra-long final as compared to other finals for the letter /e. This happens when an intrusive thought distracts the author who continues to move the sharpie forward on the paper without realizing it.

The final chapter

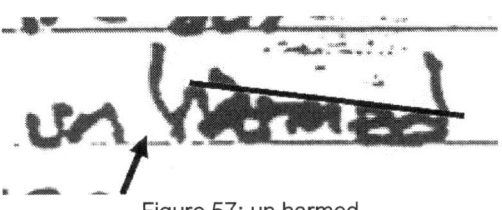

Figure 57: un harmed

The word "unharmed" has two remarkable features. The word "un" is separated from "harmed". This is again an intrusive thought while the pen moved forward floating over the paper. The "harmed" portion cramps up and the letters become smaller and get closer to each other. Words become cramped when writing muscles tense up due to an increase in anxiety. The word "unharmed" has a negative emotional impact on the writer.

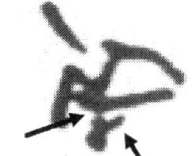

Figure 58: if distortion

The word "if" in the sentence, "if you want her to see 1997" is severely distorted. The stem of the /f is broken, the horizontal bar is disproportionally long, the i-dot is suddenly slashed. The upward stroke from the bottom of the stem does not belong. The author is so tense, she could not lift her pen upward to move toward the next stroke. The thought about whether JonBenét would be seeing 1997 had an enormous negative impact revealing her anxiety. This suggests the author knew she was not going to see 1997. We conclude the note was written after her demise by a tormented Patsy.

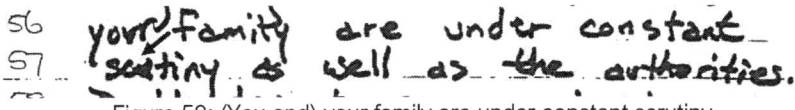

Figure 59: (You and) your family are under constant scrutiny

In line 57, we see the word "scrutiny" cramping up. The word is so distorted, it looks like the /r and /u merged or the /r is missing. This too shows the negative emotional impact the word has on the author. The thought of constant scrutiny may have been a projection as the Ramseys realized they will be scrutinized for a long time. To a kidnapper, the word scrutiny means power and control and the word would more likely expand instead of contract.

In sum:

Emotional impact analysis shows the author was attached to the victim. The emotional Patsy is more likely than the stoic John. The emotional disturbances in the writing do not match a cold-hearted intruder calmly sitting down writing a two-and-a-half-page ransom with the parents sleeping upstairs.

Fabrication

The ransom note is not only long, odd, and rambling. Certain sentences provide unnecessary information inferring fabrication.

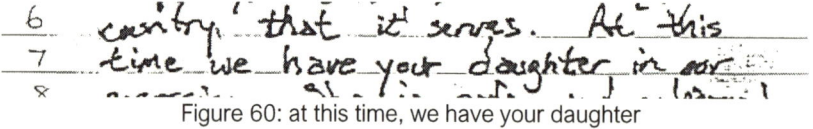
Figure 60: at this time, we have your daughter

The first hint is in the line, "at this time we have your daughter". The phrasing, "at this time" is redundant because saying, "we have your daughter" includes having her "at this time". Second, "at this time" is a finite time frame. "We have your daughter" would be an open-ended statement and more threatening. The same exaggeration is seen in, "we have your daughter in our posession[sic]". The verb "have" is a possession condition. This author is not living the kidnapping experience and not thinking with great clarity either.

The note was addressed to Mr. Ramsey. "If you want her to see 1997" is a peculiar way of addressing his need to see his daughter. The sentence portrays the perspective of the child and not that of a parent wanting their child back. It makes by far more sense to say, "if you want to see her in 1997". The sentence sequence, "her to see" versus "to see her" is a subtle and telltale sign of fabrication.

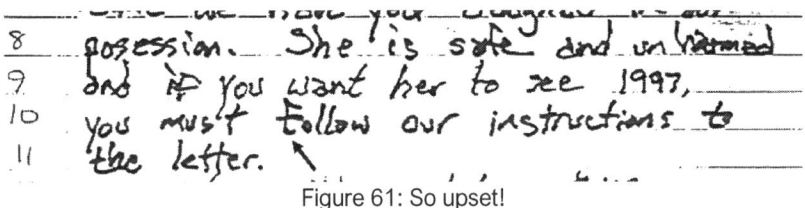

Figure 61: So upset!

The word "follow" received a horizontal bar that does not belong. The author probably wrote a /t and corrected it to an /f. It appears the author was so upset that the /t in "follow" is the start of writing "to the letter". It appears the author initially failed to write "follow instructions". The anxiety level was extremely high comes as no surprise just having gone through a major upheaval. This confusion and distraction support the anxiety seen in the word "un harmed" and the sentence, "if you want her to see 1997". Besides, 1997 was only six days away. This is a very short period for a kidnap-for-ransom situation.

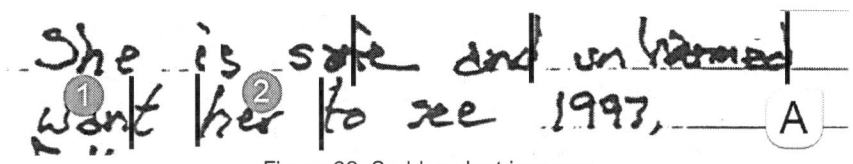

Figure 62: Sudden slant increase

The sentence, "if you want her to see 1997" is so sensitive, the author became more reactive as evidenced in the slant increase. The original drawn vertical slant at "A" is copied and pasted in various places. The enormous slant increase in the /t, /h, and /t show the author was overwhelmed and over-reactive.

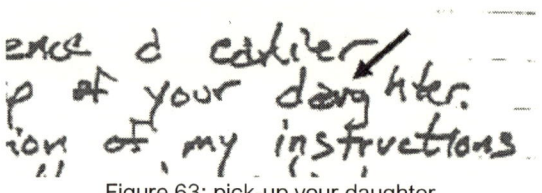

Figure 63: pick-up your daughter

We see the same cramping up and negative emotional impact in the line "your daughter". Notice the cramping up followed by extra spacing as the author lost control. "Daughter" is a word reflecting on a relationship status. This is personal and hurts when you know she is harmed.

This brings us to another common phenomenon. Exaggeration is used to convince us of the opposite. "Thou protests too much" comes to mind.

40. If we catch you talking
41. to a stray dog, she dies.
42. If you alert bank authorities, she dies.
43. If the money is in any way
44. marked or tampered with, she
45. dies. You will be scanned for
46. electronic devices and if any are
47. found, she dies.

The passage in lines 40-47 states, "she dies" four times. The exaggeration lies in the repetitiveness. This obsessive-compulsive way is trying to convince the reader she will die. Patsy attempts to convince the investigators and not John. He already knows. She is using the present tense and repetition to show JonBenét is still alive. The pretend kidnappers used, "she dies" for alibi-building. Her body was supposed to be removed from the home to be later found outside. The duct tape on her mouth made it look like the kidnappers had to keep an alive child quiet and consequently implied she was killed at a later time.

A pattern of emotional impact emerged and fabrication now makes sense:

- un harmed.
  - negative emotional impact.
  - implies the child is harmed.
- "If".
  - Severe distortions.
  - Implies she will not see 1997.
- "if you want her to see 1997".
  - Written from the child's perspective.
  - Implies she will not see 1997.
- "daughter".
  - Cramping up, increased anxiety.
  - Implies she is hurt.
- "she dies" four times.
  - Attempts to convince she is alive.
  - Implies she is dead.

The author knew the child was dead at the time of the writing. The reason why the note was written in the home makes perfect sense. JonBenét's demise was not anticipated. John's word selection confirmed her death was accidental in his CNN interview on January 1st, 1997. According to John, the alleged murder was a mere "tragedy". Ergo, he only wanted to know "why" it happened.

In sum:
Handwriting analysis reveals the author was emotionally impacted. Other phrases imply fabrication while the obsessive "she dies" and other death threats are an attempt to convince she is still alive.

No intruder
The main reason behind the intruder theory seems to be a staunch belief the parents could not have done it. They tend to be people

who cannot imagine themselves murdering their child and project their perspective on the Ramseys and relate to their plea.

Multiple examples of infanticide exist and are frequently based on a psychotic break. Former housekeeper Linda Hoffman Pugh told the Grand Jury she believed Patsy had multiple personalities. She explained she would be in a good mood and then suddenly cranky. She had never seen Patsy so upset over an argument over a dress or a friend visiting. Although the housekeeper was not in a position to diagnose, her experiences suggest Patsy may have been close to a breakdown and an accident may have happened.

A basic summary highlighting the known circumstances incompatible with the intruder theory:

1. The long ransom note was written in the home.
2. The kidnapper was at ease in the home.
3. The kidnapper left JonBenét's body behind.

The intruder theory makes no sense. The intruder was in a high-risk venture for no gain by leaving the body behind and shows the intention and known behaviors oppose each other.

Some claim the intruder had a key and spent hours in the home. He meticulously avoided leaving any trace of his presence behind and then decided to introduce himself in a lengthy ransom note. He included an introduction, praised John's business, and left an identifying clue behind in the form of an acronym. Moreover, in a leap of faith and coincidence, he owned the same handwriting characteristics and linguistics as one of the parents in the home in a one in a billion chance.

There are far more efficient ways to accomplish a kidnapping or a murder. The blow to the head or use of the alleged stun gun runs the risk of a screaming child awakening her parents. A kidnapper planning an abduction would bring chloroform to quietly subdue the child. If the objective was murder, a gun with a silencer would have sufficed. The objective of the intruder was not abduction nor murder as the behaviors and motivation contradict each other. The events that night were not anticipated and accidental.

The intruder theorists need to explain why he took the time to stage the body, write a two-and-a-half-page ransom note, and did not take the time to remove the body from the crime scene. The need for money may explain the ransom note but not the length of the note nor leaving the body behind. An intruder with the main objective to gain money would prioritize removing the body to maintain leverage over the Ramseys. We can conclude with certainty there was no intruder. Ergo, the Ramseys, as the only ones in the home, are involved.

Locard's principle
There was zero evidence an intruder was in the home and Locard's principle applies. It always has, it always will.

Dr. Edmond Locard (1877–1966) was a pioneer in forensic science who became known as the Sherlock Holmes of France. He formulated the basic principle of forensic science as: "Every contact leaves a trace".
"In forensic science (Wikipedia n.d.), Locard's principle holds that the perpetrator of a crime will bring something into the crime scene and leave with something from it and that both can be used as forensic evidence".

Locard's principle begs the question, "did the Ramseys willfully and deliberately contaminate the crime scene?" From their belief system, an intruder was present, we expect they would not make it more difficult for investigators to identify an intruder.

Ramsey's intruder theory makes no sense. John Ramsey said all doors were locked. An alternative point of entry had to be assigned to cover this irreversible statement made to law enforcement. The Ramseys honed in on a broken basement window with a scuff mark on the wall. They claimed the intruder came in through that broken window and used the strategically placed suitcase underneath as a step stool to climb out again. The suitcase, virtually empty, would have toppled with a push-off toward the small basement window. This theory is demonstrably false for several reasons.

First, John Ramsey admitted to breaking the window to get in the house when he lost his keys and did not repair it. Second, Fleet White searched for JonBenét and moved the suitcase underneath the window. This fact negates the use of the suitcase as a stepping stool. The technician photographed it under the window because he did not know it was moved from its original position. Here we see once again how a crime scene is contaminated by those present. Third, the window sill had undisturbed dust and debris. At a minimum, an intruder would have been forced to sit on the window sill to gain entry. Nobody climbs through a small 18 x 30-inch window without disturbing the dust and debris.

The strongest evidence against the window as an entry point was spiderweb strands. The window-well was covered with a grate that had to be removed to gain access. The foliage around the well was undisturbed and without visible footprints. More importantly, both Sergeant Wickman and Detective Mike Everett saw at least three spiderweb strands connecting the brick well upward to the grate. Anyone lifting the grate would have broken the spider web. A new strand would not have been formed as spiders are not active in winter. This basement window was not an entry point.

One renowned Detective, who bonded and prayed every day with the Ramseys on their front lawn, wiggled the intruder theory into a whole new alternate reality. He claimed the intruder entered the home during the day with a key. He then walked around to get to know the landscape and became aware of the little room where he would later hide her body. He would also have seen a paystub with the $118,000 deferred compensation and apparently thought, "that is a good amount to demand as a ransom". After the Ramseys came home, he continued to wait until they went to bed. He then kidnapped JonBenét which turned into murder. He decided to stage the scene and write a two-and-a-half-page ransom note. Theories like these lack any veracity.

Steve Thomas and his team members spent an entire week in the home. The home was old and walking made creaking noises. At night, they spent time lying on the bed in the master suite. With the lights switched off, "the stillness was total" (Thomas 2000)[9] The doors were locked and the basement window entry point is not an option. It is unlikely an intruder entered the home and committed a violent and likely noisy crime without being noticed. He then carried her body to the basement, staged the strangulation scene, and took his time to write a two-and-a-half-page ransom note. John, Patsy, nor Burke heard anything. Lastly, this intruder did not leave any evidence other than the ransom note behind.

This alleged intruder took his time to write a lengthy ransom note which turned to be invaluable. Place yourself in the shoes of the author and read between the lines. Handwriting comparison analysis and linguistics told us who wrote the note. The message told us why the note was written and context hinted at what happened that night.

---

[9] Page 193

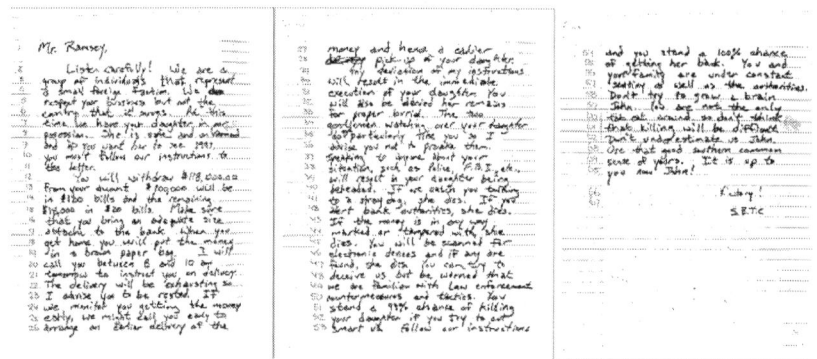

Figure 64: two-and-a-half pages, 67 lines

The ransom note is extraordinary long. And, as we will see later, was written in the home after the child's demise. There is only one case we know of which has such a long ransom note, unlike all other cases. And that case is the JonBenét Ramsey case.

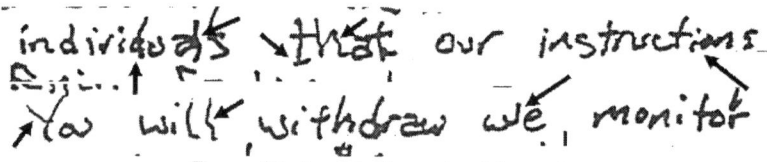

Figure 65: Anxiety throughout the note

The author has significant anxiety traits throughout the note. And that is an important clue because a kidnapper who calmly sits down to write a long ransom note takes his time and is at ease in the home. The anxiety in the handwriting does not match a calm and collected murderer. The intruder theory is absurd and built on an improbable sequence of unlikely farfetched events.

John Ramsey will prolong the intruder theory ad infinitum despite a reported and sealed plea agreement. Psychotherapist and trial consultant Laurence Smith was informed in July 2015 by an investigator that Patsy admitted to a staircase accident in exchange for not being prosecuted. JonBenét fell down the stairs and landed on "some small object" fracturing her skull. In an emotionally charged event like this, you would know exactly what

96

she fell on and specify that object. He continued with, "the truthfulness of this confession is dubious at best".

And this brings us back to the District Attorney's office treating the Ramseys with kid gloves, demanding proof beyond a reasonable doubt, stonewalling the investigative team, and using the media to misdirect and sway public opinion. The plea may explain the District Attorney Alex Hunter knew all along what happened and decided to protect the Ramseys. The hiring of Lou Smit and John Douglas may have been to use their reputation to sway public opinion. The whole District Attorney's Office seems to have a structured and disciplined plan of action. It would explain why Lou Smit, a reputable detective hired by the District Attorney, clung to a demonstrably false intruder theory. And could explain the inexplicable Mary Lacy exoneration letter and why District Attorney Alex Hunter labeled his decision to summon a Grand Jury or not as "political". "It takes a village to cover up transgressions" comes to mind.

In sum:
   a. The basement window as an entry point is impossible.
   b. There is zero evidence for the intruder theory.
   c. The Ramseys appear to deliberately contaminate the crime scene.
   d. Doors were locked.
   e. The anxiety in the handwriting does not match the coolness of a kidnapper.
   f. The violent noisy crime went unnoticed.

Locard's principle and the contradiction in known behaviors and motivation tell us there was no intruder. The intrude theory is riddled with self-defeating logic and far-fetched circumstances.

Motivation

John's behavior

The Ramseys did not behave like parents who lost a child to a kidnapper turned murderer. John Ramsey's behavioral pattern suggested he knew what happened and was unwilling to tell. John Ramsey lost his daughter, Beth, due to a car accident in 1992. John was lost and was heard wailing at night. He surrounded himself with Beth's pictures and placed her name on his plane. This is the behavior of a grieving parent we expect. According to Detective Arndt, John was "cordial" and did not console his wife about JonBenét. This is quite the opposite behavior of how he grieved for Beth.

John was missing for about an hour. Detective Arndt noticed a change in his behavior when he returned. "Whereas he had been calm and collected earlier he now sat alone in the dining room, preoccupied in thought, his leg bouncing nervously". (Thomas 2000). The stoic attitude and increase in anxiety suggest he knew what was going on and inner conflict.

Barbara Walters interviewed John Ramsey and he made the following statements:
"To those of you who may want to ask let me address very directly, I did not kill my daughter JonBenét. Uh … There have also been innuendos that she has … has been or was sexually molested. I can tell you those were the most hurtful innuendos to us as a family. Uh ... They are totally false. Uh ... JonBenai [sic: he mispronounced], …JonBenét and I had a very close relationship … uh … I will miss her dearly for the rest of my life."

Statement Analysis principles tell us the, "I did not kill my daughter JonBenét" is a strong statement. The wording "I can" is interesting as well. The word "can" be a red flag in Statement Analysis. The word "can" means that you are able but does not say you necessarily will. I can go to a store does not mean I went to the store. In that line of thinking, "I can tell you" suggests I can tell you but am I actually telling you? The word "can" weakens the assertion of a statement.

The sentence, "I can tell you those were the most hurtful innuendos" is not a denial of involvement. The next sentence, "They are totally false" reflects on the innuendos and does not negate John knowing what happened. In essence, John said, "I [John] did not kill". And that leaves the door open for Patsy.

Compare the following statements:
  (a) "There are innuendos she has been sexually molested. I can tell you those were the most hurtful innuendos to us as a family. They are false".
  (b) "The molestation innuendos are false".

The (b) sample stays on subject making it a stronger statement. Adding the sentence, "it is hurtful to us" redirects back to John and Patsy. There is no doubt it was and probably still is hurtful. The unnecessary sentence addition falls into the exaggeration to convince category.

Figure 66: John Ramsey change in behavior

John Ramsey was interviewed by Anderson Cooper (J. Ramsey 2012) and John was engaging, attentive, leaning toward Anderson, and looked him in the eye (A, A, A). There were many long pauses and he weighed his words carefully. He consistently faced Cooper but looked down when he said, "This person came into our home." At these moments, visual memories flash by. The murderer was downplayed to "a person" just like "tragedy" was a euphemism for murder.

He had a sudden and significant change in body language when asked, "Was there ever a moment you doubted your wife?"
He quickly answered, "Oh no", and turned his head away (B), "not even for a <u>nanosecond</u>. In fact, the police asked that". Turns head away again and now his voice pitched higher, "What do you think is there any possibility ..." said Anderson after which John interrupted: "...no!... none." This behavioral change is almost as strong as an admission Patsy was indeed involved.

Some sixteen years after his child's death, that question continued to make him anxious, unable to face the interviewer, and his vocal cords tightened forcing a higher pitch. The nanosecond comment also falls in the category, "exaggeration is a sign of the opposite".

A summary of his perspective and behaviors:
1. No urgency to find the killer.
2. The need to know why to move on.
3. Murder is downplayed to a tragedy.
4. A murderer is downplayed to a person.
5. He cannot face the interviewer when asked about Patsy's involvement.
6. A nanosecond is an exaggeration.

We have determined with a high degree of certainty Patsy is the author of the note and John is being protective of Patsy. They cover for each other and know what happened that night.

Early in the investigation, it was believed Patsy, "abused, tortured, and murdered" her daughter. This theory requires Patsy to be the only one involved. She would have murdered her daughter for an unclear reason, put her in the basement, staged the scene, and wrote the ransom note. John would not have been aware of his wife not coming to bed, nor recognize her handwriting or word selection. That theory does not make sense. The ransom note shows John was coerced and reveals a shift in the balance of power. If Patsy was the lone culprit with John not knowing, coercion would not have been necessary. The ransom note ended with, "It's up to you now, John!" and implies John was part of the plan and he had to decide how to move forward. Many unlikely conditions make this theory unconvincing.

In interviews, John Ramsey made conflicting statements regarding how he found JonBenét. (YouTube n.d.). In one interview he said, "I opened the door and turned the light .... sigh.... and it was her. I picked her up and I just screamed. The kind of scream that you dream, you are trying to speak but you cannot. It's just a scream".

In another interview, he was asked:
Interviewer: "When you opened the cellar door can you describe to the best of your recollections what it was that you saw".
John Ramsey: "I saw a white blanket and knew immediately I found JonBenét."
Interviewer: "Did you turn the light on?"
John Ramsey: "I don't remember turning the light on".
Interviewer: "When you found the white blanket what did you do?"
John Ramsey: "I took the tape off her mouth. I tried to untie the cord that was wrapped around her arms and I kissed her and talked to her".
Interviewer: "Did you do anything after that?"
John Ramsey: "I realized that she wasn't just asleep. That this was not good".

We have now a logical explanation for John being missing from around 11 am until noon and why Detective Arndt noticed a major change in John's behavior upon his return. He changed from being cordial and keeping to himself to nervously bouncing his leg. A behavioral change is a change in anxiety levels. Increased anxiety is a trait to protect ourselves from the fear of the unknown and the dangers lying ahead.

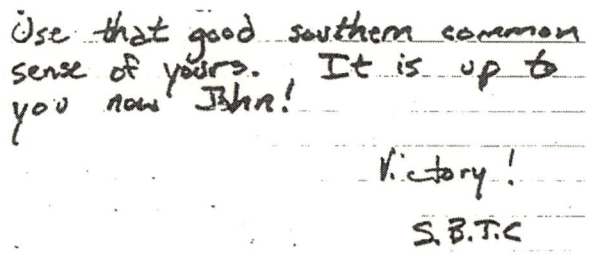

Figure 67: It is up to you now John!

According to the note, John Ramsey had a decision to make with the line, "It is all up to you now John!" John was cordial before he went missing for an hour and suggests he may have been preoccupied in thought about the decision he had to make. To tell or not to tell, that was the question.

He possibly went downstairs as he made his choice. He needed to clear his conscience and apologized for what happened to JonBenét. His choice was to protect his living cancer surviving wife and, potentially, to cover himself against an incest accusation. The apology came in the form of, "I kissed her and talked to her". Within the context of an intruder in the home, he would have opened the door, saw her, and in shock would panic, scream in disbelief, etc. But no, he said, "I kissed her and talked to her". Fleet White, who followed him to the wine cellar, heard him scream and did not reference John talking and kissing her. This suggests the kiss and talking recollection happened on a different occasion and between 11 am and noon is an excellent possibility.

Upon his return, John Ramsey was noticeably more anxious. John made his choice and faced the uncertainty of the future. He knew where JonBenét was and the increase in anxiety contributes to the idea of why he beelined to the basement.

In a 2019 interview with CNN, he was asked, "If you could say something to JonBenét now, …" (Diego 2019). John hangs his head down, and sighs. He paused for seven seconds, and said, "she knew she was loved; I told her every day I loved her, and I still do with my kids when I talk to them". Deeper sigh. "As a father, I am just sorry I did not protect her".

John Ramsey possible timeline:
- John Ramsey thinking about what to do before 11 am.
- John Ramsey made his choice around 11 am.
- John Ramsey went to JonBenét between 11 am and noon.
- John Ramsey apologized to his dead child.
- John Ramsey was highly anxious upon his return.
- John Ramsey found her body at 1 pm.
- John Ramsey told family members around 2 pm they found JonBenét at 11 am.
- John Ramsey called his pilot at 1:40 pm.

In sum:
John Ramsey's observed behaviors and collaborating circumstantial evidence tell us he knew where the body was. He likely apologized to JonBenét for her being wronged and paid with her life. This setting fits the theory both parents knew what happened and both are involved.

Dictionary
The investigation moved forward and the investigative team contacted Don Foster, an esteemed linguistic professor at Vassar College in upstate New York. He discovered the author of Primary Colors and assisted in identifying the Unabomber.

Don Foster says, "we cannot falsify who we are. Sentence structure, word usage, and identifying features can be a signature." Our environments like books, sports, hobbies, and coworkers, etc. shape us, and the words we relate to the most become our own. The Dutch and British culture has many phrases that include sailing like "Taking the wind out of my sail" while Eskimos have forty-seven words for snow.

We tend to return to what is familiar to us for the simple reason it requires less energy. And like anything else in life, people develop certain patterns and repeat them over and over again. This applies to all aspects of life whether it is selecting food, clothes, writing style, the type of friends, or your internal dictionary.

Don Foster says language is infinitely diverse and, just like no two authors write exactly the same, no two people use language the same way. There are differences in culture, sentence construction, vocabulary, spelling, punctuation, etc. Foster stated accurately, "individuals are prisoners of their own language".

We are influenced by our environment and learn from it. To understand someone, we like to know what he or she is influenced by. In that vein, Don Foster requested a list of book titles to discover influences that may match the language used by the author of the ransom note.

Quoting Steve Thomas (Thomas 2000)[10], "Then, while reviewing a list of book titles from the Ramsey home at the request of Don Foster, I dug out the Polaroid photographs from the Evidence Room. Using magnifying glasses, evidence tech Pat Peck and I compared the titles on the list with what the pictures showed. Entire shelves of books had been overlooked. When we checked the photos from a big manila envelope marked as evidence item #85KKY, I almost fell out of my chair, and Peck inhaled in sharp surprise. A picture showed Webster's New Collegiate Dictionary on a coffee table in the first-floor study, the corner of the lower left-hand page sharply creased and pointing like an arrow to the word

---

[10] Page 263

incest. Somebody had apparently been looking for a definition of sexual contact between family members. Ever so slowly, our accumulated circumstantial evidence grew."

And now a door opened to possible motivation. It is unlikely adults would leave a dictionary open on Christmas day pointing to incest while friends may visit to wish you happiness. This suggests a recent use of the dictionary as well as an anxiety situation.

The collegiate Merriam-Webster definition of incest is, "sexual intercourse between persons so closely related that they are forbidden by law to marry." Another definition is, "the statutory crime of such a relationship". The question is, "Why did an adult look up the definition of incest?" The dogearing of the page to point at the word is willful and deliberate. It seems someone looked up the definition to see whether an observed behavior fits the definition or not.

There has been an alternative theory floating around for years regarding a pedophile ring. Perry Freeman (Perry Freeman 2020), a former Colorado Springs Police Department Homicide Detective, talked about an anonymous phone call he received about a month after JonBenét's death. A stern male voice told the Detective that JonBenét was the victim of a powerful pedophile ring. She was accidentally killed using a garrote. This was the introduction to the pedophile ring and it came out of nowhere.

The phone call is of interest because the garrote was not known to the public. The caller said her passing was accidental but the garrote placement was certainly deliberate. This suggests the caller probably knew about an accidental event other than the garrote. The blow to her head with a heavy object comes to mind. Evidence suggests the hit to the head came first and made the garrote not necessary. The call was an introduction to a possible pedophile ring. Mr. Freeman mentioned the existence of pedophilia and sex trafficking in the Boulder area. The caller may have been correct; however, it is mere hearsay without any corroborating evidence. For now, the question is, "who benefits the most from this call?"

The Ramseys benefit the most as the call thwarts the investigation into a new direction. The introduction of pedophilia would explain and cover up the vaginal mucosa congestion. The Ramsey's modus operandi included evasion, misdirection, and public opinion manipulation. My thoughts regarding potential callers from most likely to least likely are:

1. John Ramsey called himself.
   a. He called Colorado Springs because Boulder Police would recognize his voice.
2. A member of the Ramsey defense team called.
   a. The Ramseys instructed them about the garrote.
3. An attention seeker in need of his 15 seconds of fame.
   a. He would not have known about the garrote.
4. An insider in a pedophile ring.
   a. There was no intruder and makes this unlikely.
5. An undercover cop who infiltrated the pedophile ring.
   a. An officer talk to Boulder Police Department directly.

There is zero evidence of an intruder. Patsy matches the handwriting of the ransom note author. The Ramsey's were reluctant to cooperate. John Ramsey pushed the pedophile theory on several occasions.

It is no surprise to me no follow-up was done regarding this phone call. The call is interesting but falls in the conspiracy theory category until hard evidence has been presented.

John Ramsey being the caller is a compelling thought. He needed to throw the Boulder Police Department off and divert attention away from themselves. The Ramsey's Modus Operandi was to distract, evade, and divert right from the start. To me, there is a good likelihood the call was made by John Ramsey or someone from the Ramsey defense team.

The coroner's report was dated December 27, 1996. The Ramseys, in their need to explain chronic vaginal inflammation, had to come up with a plausible explanation and a pedophile attending the pageants is a fit. The problem lies in the word chronic. A pedophile would not have had easy access to repeatedly visit JonBenét without being noticed over time.

Unfortunately for the Ramseys, they did not realize the dictionary was left open on the coffee table and incest is between family members. A pedophile as the alleged intruder does not make sense.

Two questions remain: What happened that night? And how does the dictionary fit in?

In sum:
 a. The anonymous call was an attempt to divert.
 b. The pedophile ring was used to explain chronic vaginal inflammation.
 c. The search for the incest definition is peculiar.
 d. The dogear is intentional.
 e. The dictionary was left open in haste.

There are a multitude of reasons why someone looks up the definition of incest. For instance, something was observed and someone looked up whether it fits the definition. Does incest mean penetration? Or is inappropriate touch considered incestuous? Is a Burke-JonBenét relationship considered incest? The reason why the definition was needed is unclear but someone needed the definition for sure. John and Patsy would have known incest is between family members but possibly not the details of the definition. Family members exclude a random intruder.

Burke's behavior

Burke Ramsey has never been a significant suspect. We expect if there was any noteworthy evidence, the investigators would have pursued that angle. The parents reported Burke stayed in bed and shielded their almost 10-year-old son which is normal. They possibly made him stay in bed so he could not see what was going on. Or more importantly, not hear what both parents were saying to each other. The young child could repeat something he overheard and that was an enormous risk. He supposedly stayed in bed with all the commotion downstairs. The parents called 911, early visitors in the home, and an officer shining a flashlight into his bedroom while he pretends to be asleep. It is unlikely to not stir his curiosity and explore what is going on.

A child psychologist, who analyzed Burke's interview by police, commented it was unusual for Burke to "feel safe" given the circumstances. Burke showed little warmth to the family and lacked emotion to the point of indifference. His behavior was interpreted as similar to children who feel they cannot, or should not, tell what happened.

Burke also commented he was, "getting on with my life" which seems a very adult thing to say. Like Don Foster, the linguistic professor, I strongly believe we are influenced by our environment. We adopt language from what we hear and read. Burke possibly repeated a comment he overheard from his parents.

Dr. Phil interviewed Burke in October 2018 and this was his first public appearance. Burke was tense, anxious, and did not like the limelight. Dr. Phil described Burke as having lived in hiding and his social skills were underdeveloped. Burke's answers to significant questions were patently strong. Dr. Phil commented, "there are still people that believe that you killed your sister and your parents covered it up to protect you". Burke replied with "Look at the evidence or the lack thereof". Dr. Phil continued with the suggestion the parents fabricated the ransom note to not lose two children. Burke hesitated with, "I...I...I do not know why they say that because "I know that is not what happened".

The initial hesitation suggests an increase in anxiety which is a red flag. The statement, "I know that is not what happened" is strong and significant. The word "that" implies distancing from knowing what happened and opens the door to Burke knowing what happened. While uttering this sentence, Burke stared straight-down in front of him. People stare or close their eyes to reduce distractions while they are pulling from their visual memory. He was potentially picturing what happened.

Dr. Phil: "Did you do anything to harm your sister JonBenét?"
Burke: "No."
Dr. Phil: "Did you murder your sister JonBenét?"
Burke: "No" (and shakes his head no).

In the same interview, Burke stated, "They won't find any evidence because that is not what happened. I know I did not do it". These are strong denials. Short and to the point. One caveat is, after years of scrutiny, he may have practiced to answer like that.

Dr. Phil was holding up the ransom note and asked whether it was his mother's writing. Burke did not provide a straightforward answer. Instead, he nervously commented about how his mother would always correct his writing to make it look better. The ransom note was "messy" and Burke implied it could not be Patsy's handwriting. Unlike some other answers, Burke did not deny it was not his mother's writing. Again, and as always, exaggeration is a method to convince the opposite. Burke knows it is Patsy's writing.

109

We need to acknowledge the Ramseys covered something up. Their behavior could have been to protect Burke. In that case, Patsy's mother instinct kicked in and John was not on board initially. The parent's behavior and comments like "why this happened", "tragedy", and the dictionary search for the definition of incest befits protecting Burke as well. Did one of the parents look it up to see whether child-to-child sexual contact is included in the definition of incest?

Burke was prepubescent and the vaginal injuries were determined to be chronic suggesting sexual contact, if there was any, happened over a period of time. We can argue the point the injuries had a different cause other than sexual contact like rough cleaning practices. Assuming Burke accidentally killed her without sexual contact, we have to ask, "why was the dictionary left open pointing at the word incest?" Why was that so important to know? And if it was Burke, where did he learn about sexual contact? Did Burke do it and the District Attorney Office knew all along? Is that why otherwise reputable investigators put their reputation on the line by sticking to a demonstrably false intruder theory?

The parents covered something up and Burke was never on the suspect list. Patsy appeared to have coerced John into cooperation. The note was addressed to John Ramsey and the phrase, "talk about your situation" is referencing a situation personal to John. Another fact is the significant change in John's behavior upon his return from being missing and during the Anderson Cooper interview. When asked about the possible involvement of his wife, he suddenly looked away and said, "not even a nanosecond". The increase in anxiety typically happens when a question comes too close to the truth and feels indefensible. The conclusions Patsy wrote the ransom note and somebody looking up the definition suggest the Ramseys were covering something very significant up for a family member.

110

Patsy became unglued when Detective Haney pressed her about her involvement. Her overreaction once again is trying to convince others through sheer force:

1. Totally impossible!
2. Go back to the drawing board!
3. "I would knock his [John Ramsey] block off"

The combination of Patsy writing the note, convincing John to cooperate, the search for the definition, and pointing to not talking about "your [John's] situation" is a compelling argument for Patsy and John keeping each other in check. Patsy accidentally killed JonBenét and John stood to be accused of incest.

It seems the scenario where Patsy accidentally struck JonBenét is a stronger motivation to coerce John into cooperation than covering for Burke. He was nine years old and would have been charged as a child. They may not have been able to prosecute him or he would have received leniency. The Ramseys would have been told by their team of lawyers. We expect they would have come clean to remove doubt and scrutiny if Burke accidentally killed his sister.

In sum:
- John exaggerated his protection for Patsy.
- Patsy's denials were not convincing.
- Team Ramsey would have advised the Ramseys about the limited law ramifications for a 9-year-old.
- Burke was never a significant suspect.
- Burke had strong denials.

In my opinion, this likely excludes Burke and once again points to the adults in the household. Patsy striking at John and accidentally hitting JonBenét is a viable option. We never stray far away from that what we know. In duress, Patsy blurted out, "I would knock his

111

[John's] block off" which may very well be linked to what happened. We may never know all the details about what happened. One day a diary may show up. One day somebody who knows may talk. And I believe Burke knows.

What we know

The Ramseys reported they spent December 25th having dinner with friends. They came home around 10 pm and John carried the sleeping JonBenét upstairs. John read to both kids which he later denied. They had an early flight the next morning and went to bed around 10:30 pm. They woke up around 5:30 am. Patsy walked down the spiral staircase and found the ransom note on one of the last steps. She alerted John and called 911 at 5:52 or about 22 minutes later. They called despite the numerous death threats and being warned they are monitored.

It is curious the note was on the third step of the stairs and a convenient height for Patsy's height but not for John who was taller. John's fingerprints were not on the note and suggest an awkward bend-over position to read. It is more likely John knew the content and had no need to read it. Patsy also stated that "the intruder must have known I [Patsy] comes down these stairs". This is incongruent with the fact the letter was addressed to "Mr. Ramsey" suggesting he was the one who should find it as the man of the house being addressed.

The Ramseys called their neighbors and they arrived shortly to roam freely through the home. Patsy told Barbara Fernie "something terrible had happened". This is of course true; however, we never veer far away from what we know to be true and this statement also downplays their position JonBenét was kidnapped. The simple reasons people do not want to lie are visible anxiety traits and being caught in a lie. Therefore, most people lie using a true statement while omitting important details.

It seems inviting friends, supposedly for support, was a deliberate and willful attempt to contaminate the crime scene and distract law enforcement, and minimized contact through distraction. Let us face some realities:

- The kidnapping is a family and police matter to resolve
- There was no forced entry and the twelve people with a key to their home are automatically in the suspect pool. A parent of an abducted child would keep them away.

Fleet White searched the basement and moved a suitcase below the basement window. Sergeant Paul Reichenbach arrived and searched the home as did John Ramsey. The doors were locked. They found no signs of forced entry and did not see evidence of a struggle. The alarm system was reportedly not engaged which is odd. John Ramsey said in an interview he checked the alarm before going to bed. That seems a normal habit to do.

In the 911 call Patsy said, "We just got up" and in an interview stated she went downstairs to make coffee. Officer French arrived within three minutes and Patsy opened the door fully dressed with hair and makeup intact. It turned out she wore the same black pants and red turtleneck as the day before. The Ramseys started lawyering up by 7:30 am. The Ramseys claimed Burke slept through it all. Officer French mentioned to Sergeant Reichenbach that, "something is not right".

Detective Arndt arrived at 8:10 am. Patsy told Officer French she checked the bedroom before she found the note and told Detective Arndt, she found the note and then checked the bedroom. Detective Arndt reported John Ramsey was calm, composed, and "cordial". Oddly, Patsy and John did not console each other during this difficult time not knowing where their daughter was. John stayed in the den while Patsy stayed in the sunroom. The ransom note specified, "I will call you between 8 and

10 am tomorrow". The unusual long-time frame came and went. Nobody paid attention to the phone.

Detective Arndt reported John Ramsey was missing for an hour from around 11 am till noon. She thought he got the mail and was reading it and did not realize they received mail in a slot in the house. He would not have to go outside to pick up the mail. She noted a remarkable change in behavior upon his return as John was anxiously bouncing his leg up and down.

Detective Arndt, now alone with multiple adults free to go where they wanted, had no way to control them. She called for assistance on her cellphone as radio silence was ordered but did not receive assistance. Next, she made a poor judgment call and asked John Ramsey and Fleet White to search the home from top to bottom and leave evidence where it was. She effectively deputized civilians without knowing she could put them in harm's way if an armed intruder was still in the home.

John beelined to the little room in the basement where he found JonBenét at 1:05 pm. She was wrapped in a white blanket. Fleet White testified he believed John knew where she was. He also stated John screamed before he switched the light on. John pulled the duct tape off her mouth and left it in the little room. Despite the panicked commotion Fleet White caused by running upstairs about having found the body, Patsy Ramsey stayed in the sunroom and did not attempt to meet her daughter. John Ramsey carried her lifeless body, in full rigor mortis, upstairs and laid her on the floor. Detective Arndt checked for a pulse, smelled the odor of decay, and told John she had passed. He was crying but Arndt did not see any tears. Their eyes locked and Arndt had the feeling John knew what had happened.

The crime scene changed from a kidnapping to a murder scene. Detective Arndt called in for a coroner and further assistance.

The final chapter

Crime scene technicians and victim advocates arrived. John told victim advocate Grace Morlock that he did not think the killer meant to kill JonBenét because she was wrapped in a blanket.

John Ramsey called his pilot at 1:40 pm, just 35 minutes after he discovered his daughter's body. He ordered him to get the plane ready for them to fly to Atlanta to spend Christmas with his older children from a previous marriage. Law enforcement prevented their departure and thought it was odd he readied himself to leave. It is incomprehensible for a father who "just learned" about the death of his daughter to leave her behind. John did not want to avail himself to investigators in this murder scene.

John Andrew Ramsey and Belinda Ramsey, John's children from a previous marriage, arrived by taxi from the airport at 2:15 pm. Belinda's fiancé Stewart Long accompanied them. During an interview, Stewart Long informed Detectives that John Ramsey told them JonBenét was with Beth [context: heaven] now and they discovered her body at 11 am. The time frame was a striking Freudian slip as John found the body with Fleet White at 1:05 pm. It is no coincidence John was missing from about 11 am until noon. John Ramsey likely visited and/or moved her body in that time frame and he misspoke.

In sum:
    a. 911 call showed a lack of urgency on Patsy's part.
    b. John Ramsey was cordial.
    c. The Ramseys lawyered up early.
    d. The Ramseys were minimally cooperative.
    e. Patsy was inconsistent about finding the ransom note.
    f. The Ramseys did not pay attention to the expected call.
    g. John beelined to the basement.
    h. John called his private pilot to leave the murder scene.
    i. John tells misspoke about the time finding JonBenét.

The hidden message

There were three people in the home: John, Patsy, and Burke. It is a widely held opinion Patsy wrote the ransom note and we are moving forward with this perspective. The two-and-a-half-page ransom note was written after JonBenét's death and the scene was staged. The ransom note was signed S.B.T.C [no period].

A dictionary had a page dogeared pointing to the word "incest". The coroner determined chronic vaginal abuse. We need to have a look at the ransom note as a whole and how the dictionary fits in the storyline.

The ransom note has a veiled message and requires us to read in between the lines. We hunt for hints, clues, and double meanings. Remember, "People say exactly what they mean" and it is up to the investigators to figure out what they meant.

Exaggeration is a sign of the opposite. The long-winded ransom note points to a very significant event to have taken place to require an excessive and elaborate coverup. And that begs the question: What was so significant that an elaborate coverup outweighed their daughter's demise? What were they so afraid of that they chose a coverup over bringer JonBenét to a hospital?

The note was addressed to Mr. Ramsey and he needed to "Listen carefully!" The note was written by someone who did not experience a kidnapping event. The note shows 72% of the text describing the event and 59% are threats. These exaggerations imply deceit.

Patsy had to convince investigators a kidnapping had taken place. Patsy was a loving and caring mother and the ransom note shows us all too well she was not familiar with criminal perspectives and intentions.

Patsy is the author and therefore we can assume she was the most motivated for a cover-up. John needed convincing in order to cooperate as "Listen carefully!" implies.

Patsy must have done something significant to put this much effort into a cover-up and have the need to coerce John into cooperation. For John to let himself be coerced suggests Patsy had something of equal value hanging over John's head. There is somehow a balance of power between the two main players and they kept each other in check.

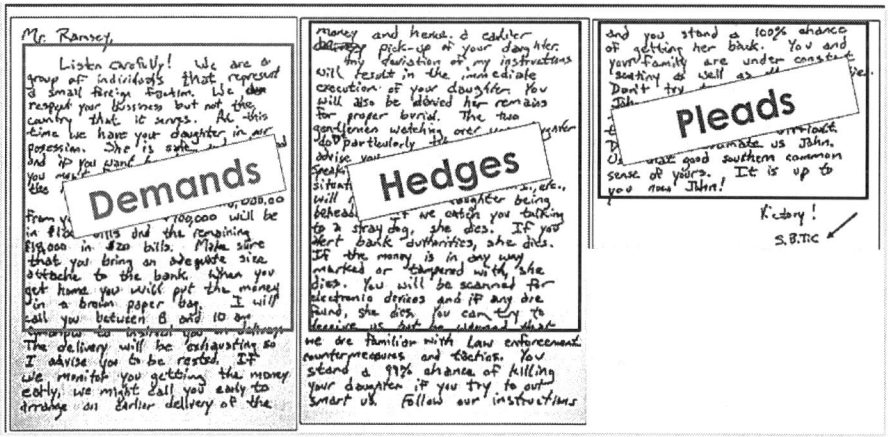

Figure 68: Three parts

The ransom note has three distinct parts which I refer to as demanding, hedging, and pleading. There is a definite "shift in the balance of power" away from Patsy and towards John.

The ransom note can be summarized as follows: In part one Patsy is demanding and insistent:

1. Mr. Ramsey.
2. **Listen** carefully! We are a
3. group of individuals that represent
4. a small foreign faction. We ~~don't~~

5. respect your business but not the
6. country that it serves. At this
7. time we have your daughter in our
8. posession [sic]. She is safe and un
harmed
9. and if you want her to see 1997,
10. you **must** follow our instructions to
11. the letter.
12. You **will** withdraw $118,000.00
13. from your account. $100,000 **will** be
14. in $100 bills and the remaining
15. $18,000 in $20 bills. **Make sure**
16. that you bring an adequate size
17. attache to the bank. When you
18. get home you **will** put the money
19. in a brown paper bag.

Patsy shows who is in charge in line 1-19. Patsy, trying to see events through the eyes of a kidnapper, does a poor job to convince with unusual demands.

The second part is a mix of threats in abundance and seemingly unnecessary advice:

19. I will
20. call you between 8 and 10 am
21. tomorrow to instruct you on delivery.
22. The delivery will be exhausting so
23. **I advise** you to be rested. **If**
24. we monitor you getting the money
25. early, we **might** call you early to
26. arrange an earlier delivery of the
27. money and hence a [sic]earlier
28. ~~delivery~~ pickup of your daughter.
29. Any deviation of my instructions

30. **will result** in the immediate
31. execution of your daughter. You
32. **will also be denied** her remains
33. for proper burial. The two
34. **gentlemen** watching over your daughter
35. do \not/ particularly like you so I
36. **advise you** not to provoke them.
37. Speaking to anyone about your
38. situation, such as Police, F.B.I.,etc.
39. **will result** in your daughter being
40. beheaded. If we catch you talking
41. to a stray dog, **she dies**.
42. If you alert bank authorities, **she dies**.
43. If the money is in any way
44. marked or tampered with, **she**
45. **dies**. You will be scanned for
46. electronic devices and if any are
47. found, **she dies**. You can try to
48. deceive us but be warned that
49. we are familiar with law enforcement
50. countermeasures and tactics. You
51. stand a **99% chance of killing**
52. your daughter if you try to out
53. smart us. Follow our instructions
54. and you stand a 100% chance
55. of **getting her back**. You and your family
56. are under **constant**
57. **scrutiny** as well as the authorities.

Lines 19-57 show kinder language (I advise, might, gentlemen, advise you, getting her back) mixed with a multitude of varying death threats.

The third and last part finalizes the shift in the balance of power. Patsy, the demanding kidnapper, releases the reins and leaves it up to John to decide:

58. **Don't** try to **grow** a brain
59. John. You are not the only
60. fat cat around so don't think
61. that killing will be difficult.
62. **Don't underestimate** us John.
63. Use that good Southern common
64. sense of yours. **It is up to**
65. **you now John!**
66.   Victory!
67. S.B.T.C [no period]

The last paragraph is telling. Patsy switches from the formal "Mr. Ramsey" to the personal and familiar "John". She is warning John to "not grow a brain" and to "use that good Southern common sense". Patsy is more or less pleading for John not to change his mind. The last sentence explains it all. "It is up to you now John!" The exclamation mark emphasizes John is the final decision-maker and he better not mess it up. Patsy relinquished control and realized in the end John decides how he will move forward.

And that is very curious if there indeed was an intruder. No kidnapper in the world takes charge and lets John be the final decision-maker in the end. However, it makes a whole lot of sense from the perspective Patsy wrote the note.

In sum:
    a. The ransom note has a hidden message.
    b. Patsy coerced John into cooperation.

Alibi building

Ramsey's plan was fundamentally quite simple. They fabricated a kidnapping gone wrong as a cover for events they were involved in that night. The kidnapping explains the ransom note and why JonBenét was missing.

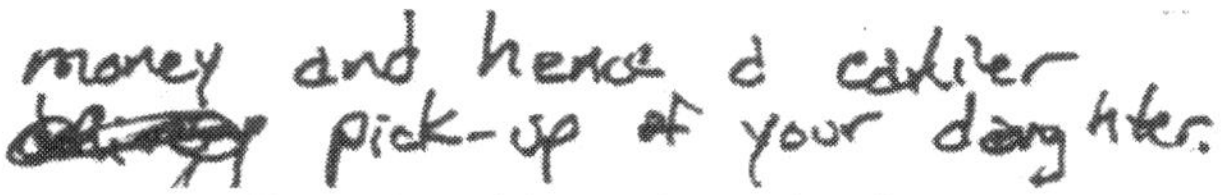

Figure 69: pick-up of your daughter

The inference of the line "pick-up of your daughter" tells us the Ramseys planned to dispose of her body outside their home. She would be found later and hopefully decomposed enough to mask their involvement once JonBenét was found. Something stopped the Ramseys from moving JonBenét to a different location and she remained in the cellar. The duct tape on her mouth had "a perfect lip print" and implies she must have been unconscious. An intruder who left the body behind would not need to use duct tape on an unconscious or dead child.

The duct tape makes perfect sense from a fabricated storyline perspective. Her body would be found outside the home with duct tape on her mouth showing the kidnappers kept an alive child quiet. JonBenét was then supposedly killed later with a garrote after a botched delivery of the money. The line, "do not think killing will be difficult" is a threat from the kidnapper's perspective. For John and Patsy, the same line represents what already happened. Incidentally, the phrase "fat cat" is reportedly a very Southern thing to say matching Patsy's stomping ground.

Word selection is paramount and may not fit the circumstance. It will reveal the author's perspective and potential motivation. People often say things that do not fit the context and such Freudian slips are called "leakage".

The language used in the ransom note is a mixture of demands with emotional and abstract threats. The change in tone is curious as it appears John partially assisted Patsy in writing the ransom note. There are word characteristics John seemed involved with and influenced the content. John, unlike Patsy, used expressions like chance and percentages in interviews. Words like monitor, execution, electronic device, and scanned are computer terms John would frequently use as the CEO of Access Graphics. The word selection suggests he was actively involved in writing the note and in the planning for the removal of her body.

This brings me back to the unusual phrases of concern for the father of the victim, the unusual instructions, and the excessive threats about the child not returning alive.

- Make sure you bring an adequate size attaché to the bank
- Put the money in a brown paper bag
- I will call you between 8 and 10 tomorrow to instruct
- The execution of your daughter, beheaded and dies x 4
- You will also be denied her remains
- Don't think killing will be difficult

The assumption is we talk about what is important to us or what we relate to the most. Regardless of what is expressed, the first and foremost question is always, "why was this important enough to mention?" The subjects addressed must have significance to Patsy and John otherwise they would not be in the ransom note. The answer is once again quite simple: alibi building.

1. The ransom note is addressed to Mr. Ramsey as he was to execute the plan. He would place her body in a suitcase and hide her elsewhere. The adequate attaché is probably a reference for transporting the body. It appears an instruction however it is meant as a cover in case John was

seen in public hauling a larger suitcase in the early hours on December 26th.

2. The duct tape, part of the garrote cord, and the other half of the broken paintbrush were not found. The line "you will put the money in a brown paper bag" is specific and unnecessary. This can be a cover in case John was seen disposing of these items because the bag would not be strong enough to hold the weight of the money.

3. The unusual time frame, between 8 and 10 am, allows for time to dispose of the body. The act of going to the bank makes it look like the Ramseys were fearful and chose to follow "the instructions to the letter".

4. The above scenario provided the Ramseys an excuse to leave the home, have a reason to be seen with an attaché, and explains why they did not call the police immediately. They could delay reporting until after 10 am.

5. The excessive death threats were written to enforce the appearance the Ramseys were fearful and forced to follow the instructions. The other side of the coin is to convince law enforcement the child was still alive.

6. The "you will also be denied her remains" is the cover of why JonBenét would not be returned if not found in a hiding place outside the home. The Ramseys knew she was dead and is eerily similar to Patsy using, "our daughter is gone" in the 911 call.

7. The line, "You're not the only fat cat around" and "don't think killing will be difficult" supports the idea the Ramseys wrote the ransom note after JonBenét's death. The "kidnappers" implied there were plenty of replacements for JonBenét as leverage for money reducing taking the child to a business transaction.

Patsy called 911 at 5:52 am in a call regarded as rehearsed and deceptive. The Ramseys were pressured to call. Investigators would have discovered they planned an early flight and wonder why they were not up early to discover their child missing. Calling long after the 10 am deadline may raise suspicion and run the risk of being labeled as uncaring parents. John and Patsy did not anticipate events that night or they would not have made travel plans for early December 26th. An accident happened and they had adversary roles and needs. It would take an estimated three to four hours to overcome disbelief, agony, arguing, plan an alternative reality, discuss how to move forward, and execute the plan. This is why Patsy's coercion of John shines through in the note. They were forced to strike a deal favorable to both.

Things went downhill from there. Fact is, JonBenét's body remained in the house. Something changed their minds regarding the removal of her body. They did not anticipate something thwarting their plan to remove her as a kidnapper would have. The reasons can range from the emotional inability to dump the body out in the elements; the bank was closed on December 26th taking away their alibi to walk around with an attaché, or rigor mortis had already set in. JonBenét's arms were stretched overhead and she did not fit into a suitcase. They could not force themselves to do what more experienced killers have done before them. They were forced to act and call 911. Decay was setting in and body odor would provide law enforcement a question they could not explain: "How come you never noticed?"

In sum:
The ransom note has a hidden meaning.
    a. Patsy needed to convince John.
    b. John assisted with the text of the ransom note.
    c. The plan to remove her body failed.
The ransom note builds an alibi.
    d) The Ramsey planned on removing JonBenét's body from the crime scene.
    e) The duct tape placement implies kidnappers kept an alive child quiet.

A viable scenario

The dogeared dictionary opened the door to logical scenarios. It is hard to imagine someone leaves an opened dictionary pointing to the word incest on Christmas day. Incest is a strong motivator to stage the scene and write the ransom note.

There were three people left in the home that could have been involved in incest. In order of statistical probability: John, Patsy, and Burke. There are a few possible scenarios, however, given the context, only one seems to be viable.

A possible scenario, yet still speculative and supported by the evidence is that Patsy accidentally killed JonBenét.

Patsy accidentally hit JonBenét

Patsy walked in on John in a compromising position with JonBenét. Patsy was already suspicious and the multitude of doctor visits may attest to that. JonBenét was a bedwetter and reportedly regressed around that time. Patsy was in the hospital with ovarian cancer the year before and the maid told her a blonde hair was found in their bed. Patsy told her, "to keep that blonde bitch down the street away from my husband" (Thomas 2000)[11].

Patsy was already on edge because of her suspicions. Patsy then recalled the blonde hair in her bed and seeing John with JonBenét instantly enraged her. She lost control and swung at John with a force to hit an adult. He instinctively evaded the blow, turned around holding JonBenét facing him. Patsy accidentally struck her daughter on the head. The crack in her skull was eight-and-a-half inches long in the shape of a Maglite. Her skull was hit on top-right suggesting a right-handed individual struck her from behind. The

---

[11] Page 82

sound of the crack, her scream, and her body instantly going limp made them believe she was dead.

Whether incest occurred or not, and there is of course no reported history is entirely irrelevant. Patsy suspected abuse took place and believed it happened at that moment. One thing is undeniable and blatantly clear. Somebody found it necessary to look up the definition of incest and somebody believed an encounter sexual in nature between family members occurred.

Incest matches the conclusion of a panel of pediatric experts who determined JonBenét suffered vaginal trauma before the day she was killed. They concluded the trauma was consistent with chronic physical abuse and can only be accomplished by someone with easy access while not being suspected.
And now a possible motive to cover up the events of that night has arisen. John and Patsy were both involved and both had something to hide. Patsy accidentally struck and killed her daughter. She survived cancer the year before and did not want to go to prison. She would run the risk of not getting the medical attention she required and feared dying during incarceration. John stood to be accused of incest, prison time, and social scrutiny.

Tom Haney, a retired Denver homicide Detective, applied pressure to Patsy during an interview in June 1998. On the third day of the interview, the "Southern Belle turned into a steel magnolia". He brought up the fact there was vaginal abuse and she demanded to see the evidence and she was "extremely" surprised and "had no idea". Always remember, when someone says, "I have no idea" they are denying having an idea. The next question should always be, "what were you thinking of?"

Patsy became outraged when Detective Haney pointed out investigators may have trace evidence linking her to JonBenét's death: "Totally impossible. Go retest it! Go back to the drawing board". Haney continued to press her and pushed the issue she may have been involved and it was probably an accident. She held her hand up like a stop sign and said, "You are going down the wrong path, buddy!" Later she said, "If John Ramsey were involved, honey, we would not be sitting here. I would have knocked his block off. Read my lips! This was not done by a family member. Did not happen. Period. End of statement." (Thomas 2000)[12]

The extremely strong denial suggests an increase in anxiety and implies exaggeration to convince. When Detective Haney suggested it may have been John, Patsy made the interesting comment: "I would have knocked his block off". We do not veer far away from what we know. Knocking his block off is what happened that night and consistent with Patsy attempting to strike John.

From this perspective, motive, means, and opportunity have an explanation and the content of the note makes a whole lot more sense. There was equilibrium in the balance of power between the two main players and they held each other in check. Patsy accidentally killed JonBenét and John had incest hanging over his head. Patsy's as the murderer is a strong motivation for her to write the note and her need to coerce John into cooperation. She did not want to end up in jail without medical care and John was motivated to avoid public scrutiny.

The Ramseys decided to cover up what happened that night and the scenario has motivating elements for both parents. The consequences of what happened that night outweighed the scrutiny over the fabricated kidnapper storyline. We can safely assume the details are not completely accurate, however, I do believe the gist is close to what happened. Patsy had something over John and John knew something about Patsy. This balance of

---

[12] Page 326

power is a compelling explanation for the meaning of the acronym S.B.T.C [sic].

The Ramseys continue to maintain the intruder theory against all odds. This is understandable from their self-preservation perspective. John has made certain statements in the past which also make sense within the context of this scenario. We never deviate far from what we know. His statements like, "it was someone who was jealous" and "someone angry with me" is assigned to an intruder and befits Patsy within this scenario.

The premise Patsy hit JonBenét accidentally is supported by the evidence and explains the motivation and their behaviors.

- John and Patsy did not prioritize JonBenét.
- Patsy rehearsed the 911 call.
- John and Patsy did not console each other.
- John called his pilot 40 minutes after he found JonBenét.
- John called the murder a tragedy.
- John wants to know why it happened.
- Patsy said, "I would knock his block off".

S.B.T.C [no period]

Patsy started the ransom note with, "Listen carefully!" The verb "listen" implies they were talking prior to writing the note. The parents must have been in shock, disbelief, and unable to think straight. She was likely trying to convince John to participate in a fabricated intruder story. It may have taken them 45 minutes to an hour or two to figure out what to do and what to agree on. JonBenét's brain swelling suggests some time had passed between the blow to the head and the staging with the garrote.

The final chapter

LINE 2 **LISTEN CAREFULLY!** This is the warning	LINE 37 **ABOUT YOUR SITUATION** The reason for the warning	Line 64 **UP TO YOU NOW JOHN!** John to decide how to proceed

Figure 70: Hidden message

"Listen carefully!" is a demand and implies Patsy is not giving John a choice. You better or else! John needed to be convinced and was initially not on board with the plan. In the middle of the note, the line, "do not speak about your situation" is interesting. Your situation seems to mean the alleged kidnapping however we know Patsy wrote the note and there was no intruder. From her perspective and the context, this line likely has a very different meaning. Your situation is likely linked to the dictionary and the word "incest". The "your situation" is associated with the addressee, Mr. Ramsey. The last line of the ransom note tells all: "It's up to you now John!" and John decides how to move forward.

The hidden message in the ransom note is quite simple when you remove superfluous information. If he tells what happened that night, Patsy's hammer will come down with equal force.

- Patsy accidentally struck JonBenét.
- Patsy did not want to go to prison for lack of medical care.
- John stands to be accused of incest.
- Both John and Patsy hold each other in check.

The balance of power moved toward John as the note came to a close. The formal "Mr. Ramsey" changed to the more intimate "John" and is in line with the pleading tone. This not only suggests familiarity, but it also softened the stand-off. The intimacy theme reared its head again as the author knew John had a link to the

South. The line "use that good Southern common sense of yours" is an appeal to not change his mind and implicates John as part of the cover-up. Patsy feared his common sense.

The fear lies in the word "that" where she distanced herself from his common sense. If John would come to his senses, there would be negative repercussions for herself. This supports the idea Patsy was the one most motivated to write the note. She, likely accidentally, killed JonBenét and knew the child was dead when writing the note.

The statements and handwriting characteristics now makes sense:

- Emotional attachment in "un harmed"
- If you want her to see 1997
- She dies x 4

58. Don't try to grow a brain suggests John had alternatives including exposing Patsy.

63. Use that good Southern common sense of yours implies Patsy feared John might tell what happened that night.

64. It is up to you now John! indicates in the end, it was John who was in charge of the only and most important decision. To tell or not tell. That is the question.

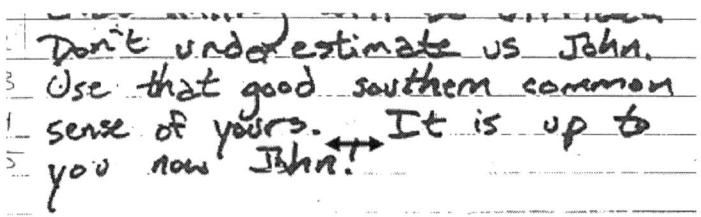

Figure 71: It is up to you now John

Patsy is insecure and hesitant about the idea of having to give up control and unsure about the eventual outcome. Intrusive thoughts widen word spacing as we see in that sentence. She is dependent on what John will do in the future. Patsy could not possibly be sure whether John would talk with authorities. That is why she demanded him to "Listen carefully!". She ended the ransom note with a word of hope: Victory!

Patsy, known to use acronyms frequently, signed with S.B.T.C [sic]. She knew she had done all she could and realized she could no longer control John's choices after finishing the ransom note and once law enforcement was called. John was now in charge and Patsy ended the note with an acronym reflecting on "whatever happens, happens". She signed the note with S.B.T.C [sic] which is, in my opinion, the natural conclusion of the note's message note:

"So Be The Case"

The explanation So Be The Case is compelling. It explains why Patsy addressed John and why there was a shift in the balance of power. And it shows both Patsy and John were involved.

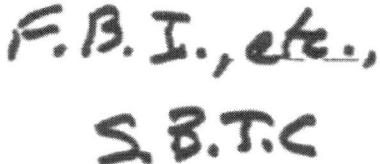

Figure 72: S.B.T.C last period missing

The ransom note has overall proper punctuation and the acronym F.B.I. received all three periods. Interestingly, the acronym S.B.T.C [no period] did not receive the last period. Habitual use of acronyms customarily does not use periods at all. Compare ASAP, IMO, and ISBN for instance. Yet, the author showed with F.B.I. periods are used and the lack of the last /C period suggests an intrusive thought distracted Patsy. A possible thought about, "what will happen next" scenarios or "will John tell or not tell?"

S.B.T.C [no period] appears to be meant to be the name of a foreign faction and implies habitual use. The missing period implies the acronym was not habitual and supports the idea it was fabricated. There was no foreign faction, no intruder, and no pedophile ring.

Patsy ended the note with "Victory!". This is probably reflecting on "we will prevail if we stick to the story" and shows hope.

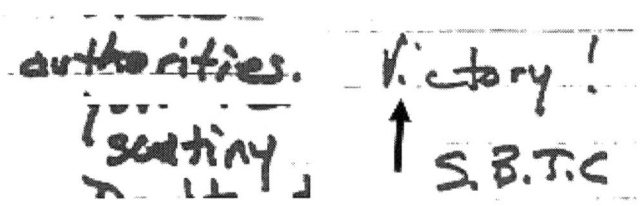

Figure 73: Victory

The word Victory has a significantly shrunken Mid-Zone-i which stays close to the /V showing Patsy is not sure her coverup will find John's continued support. The extra spacing after the Mid-Zone-i and the /c is once again an intrusive thought distracting her.

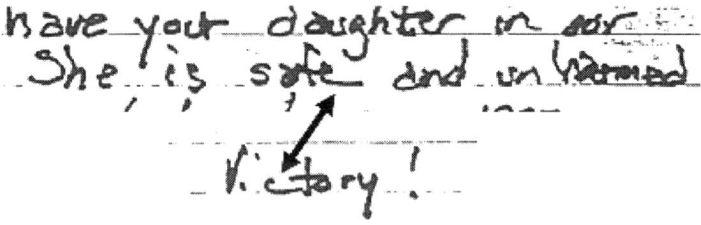

Figure 74: She is safe and victory

The /c extension is a repeat of an intrusive thought and the pen subconsciously moved forward leaving an ink trail. The smaller Mid-Zone-i, the extra spacing, and the lengthened final of the /c show insecurity. Her fate is in John's hands.

John's possible influence

The ransom note was written by Patsy as the handwriting, word selection, and lens of perspective suggest. The first one-and-a-half page is emotionally driven with an incoherent message. There is a shift in the second half on page two where the language use is more abstract and linguistically different. The change suggests John may have had some influence on the content.

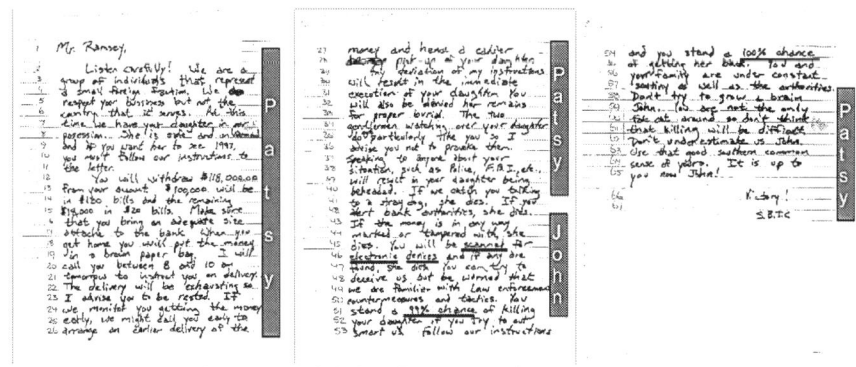

Figure 75: John's influence on the ransom note

It makes sense from the perspective Patsy swung at John and accidentally hit JonBenét. They were in shock, did not know what to do, and came up with the kidnapping plan to make sense of JonBenét not being at home.

It seems Patsy, with a major in Journalism, was assigned the task to write the ransom note while John staged the scene with the garrote. The verbiage, "if you want her to see 1997", "she dies" (x 4), and "denied her remains for proper burial" attest to JonBenét's body not going to be returned. The abrupt change in linguistics suggests John returned to Patsy who was still busy writing the note. Now the question is: "If true, returned from what?"

He probably returned from staging which was necessary as they had to ensure it looked like the child was taken and dumped after being killed. John's staging must have taken less time than Patsy writing the ransom note. John returned and could be linked to the second half of page two.

In the last paragraph, Patsy takes one last-ditch effort to regain control with "don't try to grow a brain, John". We have to wonder what John said upon his return for Patsy to warn him not to change his mind.

In sum:
1. Patsy swung at John.
2. Patsy accidentally struck JonBenét.
3. Patsy and John fabricated the kidnapping storyline.
4. Patsy coerced John into cooperation.
5. Patsy and John planned to relocate her body.
6. Patsy called 911 and is considered a rehearsed call.
7. John downplayed the murder to a tragedy.
8. John downplayed the murderer to "this person".
9. John is motivated for fear of incest accusations.
10. John stated, "I did not kill JonBenét".
11. Patsy stated, "I would knock his block off.

Alternative theories

In my opinion, the following theories presented are less likely.

Patsy was frustrated over bedwetting
One theory is Patsy struck JonBenét frustrated over bedwetting. The use of a heavy object to hit the child implies intent to damage while a slap would have sufficed. Moreover, JonBenét was hit from behind and in punishment scenarios Patsy would have faced the child. Bedwetting and frustration go together but intentionally hurting a child that bad is unexpected and unlikely.

This theory hinges on the soiled long johns and the diapers hanging out of a closet. The counter to this theory is JonBenét lost sphincter control when rendered unconscious and then soiled her pants.

Interestingly, the soiling was from the waistband down and saturation significantly more to the left thigh. This can be consistent with JonBenét lying in bed on her left side or John was holding her facing him. This would explain why the right-handed Patsy swinging at John would strike JonBenét on the right and rear of her head. John evaded the blow to his right and moved JonBenét along with him which is her left.

Patsy and rivalry
Another theory is Patsy felt that JonBenét became too close to John and saw her as a rival. This scenario has happened in the past and some claim S.B.T.C [no period] stands for "She Became Too Close". Patsy lived vicariously through JonBenét reliving her pageant days. In this case, she would stand to lose a lot.

Patsy had a psychotic break
One theory claims John Ramsey had inappropriate contact with JonBenét and Patsy dissociated from the clues. The combination of her health problems, medication, the stress of the holidays, and alcohol led her to have a psychotic break. Burke said to a child psychologist he remembered his mother going psycho. This could be possible as some say the household seemed dysfunctional with bedwetting, JonBenét not cleaning herself properly, the home in constant disorder despite having a maid. The housekeeper reportedly said that no one picked up after themselves. On the other hand, Patsy wrote the note and it seems unlikely she would be able to write a lengthy note so soon after a psychotic break. One would expect the handwriting more disorganized and undisciplined significant distortions throughout the note.

JonBenét fell down the stairs
Some suggest JonBenét fell down the stairs. She landed on an unknown object causing the skull fracture. This is highly unlikely as there would be bruising in varying places consistent with the fall. And Patsy would have known what object she had fallen on and disclosed that when needed.

Burke retaliated

There has been speculation regarding Burke having struck JonBenét and accidentally killing her. I can imagine an almost 10-year-old having a sibling rivalry and even being angered by all the attention she received. The investigative team would have found evidence pointing in Burke's direction. Burke appeared to be present during the 911 call and asked, "What did you find?" If involved, Burke would likely have cowered in his room realizing what he did was beyond bad.

Patsy started paying more attention to JonBenét and that may have been welcomed by Burke as a reserved and quiet kid. Mother focusing on JonBenét removed the pressure off Burke as mothers can be intrusive and demanding to a quiet child. Former housekeeper Linda Wilcox remarked Burke's bedwetting ceased when JonBenét got more attention.

Some presented the theory Burke had been molesting JonBenét for some time and this was a source of contention between the parents. Burke went down to play in the basement at night and was discovered by JonBenét. He may have molested her or tried to and she was going to tell the parents. He felt threatened and in anger, he hit JonBenét with a heavy object. The main reason for the anger outburst is the "evidence" Burke hit JonBenét with a golf club in the past, alleged and unproven smearing of feces. There is no evidence Burke had habitual anger issues.

Patsy discovered JonBenét hurt and did not want to tell the sleeping John. The argument is she feared he would not be able to love his son anymore. In this scenario, Patsy's mother instinct kicked in and she protected her son. She staged JonBenét's body and wrote the ransom note. There are holes in this theory and inconsistencies with the context of the situation.

Theories claiming Patsy staged and wrote the note on her own accord are likely incorrect. The lines, "do not grow a brain John" and, "use that good Southern common sense of yours" imply he knew what was going on. You can only grow a plant when you have a seed. John must have had some basic knowledge to work with to decide how to move forward: "It is up to you now John".

The most important evidence Patsy did not protect Burke is in the ransom note itself. Patsy tried to convince John with "Listen carefully!", "do not speak about your situation", and "It is all up to you now, John!" John would not need much coercion to protect his son. This also brings us back to Burke's strong answer to Dr. Phil: "I know that is not what happened". And "that" refers to Burke having killed his sister accidentally.

Brother to sister molestation at age 10 and 6 happens and is statistically rare. There is another flaw in this perspective. Typically, when a child has poor urge control at this young age and significantly oversteps boundaries, then they overstep boundaries as adults as well. Burke has no known history of abuse and overstepping boundaries in his adulthood.
Burke is a withdrawn type. They tend to be reserved, quiet, and introspective. His childhood pictures show a child seemingly meek. Burke reportedly works from home and avoids the limelight. He works in information technology and from behind a computer screen. That is a good fit for a withdrawn type and someone with, like Dr. Phil described, underdeveloped social skills. These types tend to not assert themselves strongly and think before they speak and act. At parties, they tend to keep more to themselves and you may see them sitting in a corner staring at their phone instead of socializing. His withdrawn pattern does not exclude Burke from striking JonBenét however, these types tend to withdraw during stress reactions. This is the opposite of confront and attack.

John hit JonBenét
Patsy wrote the note and coerced John into cooperation. John would not need convincing to cover up if he was the guilty party. John would have to convince Patsy instead.

JonBenét unconscious before getting home

It has been suggested that JonBenét was unconscious already when they arrived home. Part of the reasoning is John carrying her upstairs apparently asleep. The problem with this scenario is the pineapple in her stomach was consumed at home and means she was alive. The partially digested pineapple provides a clue as to the time of death. They reported coming home at 10 pm and we can safely assume they remained awake for some thirty minutes. She probably at the pineapple in that time frame. The partial digestion, let say between thirty minutes to an hour, suggests digestion was halted around 11:30 pm and explains her body to be in full rigor mortis when found at 1 pm the following afternoon.

Pedophile ring killed JonBenét

The pedophile ring theory likely started with the anonymous phone call to the Colorado Springs Police Department. The stern male voice said JonBenét was accidentally killed with a garrote and a powerful pedophile ring was involved. There is overwhelming evidence there was no intruder in the home. The spiderweb in the basement window-well told us the window was not an entry point. The intruder left zero evidence behind. Patsy would not write the note to cover for a stranger. The Ramseys contaminating the scene to obscure a random intruder is also highly unlikely.

Mismanagement

Grand Jury

Finally, in April 1998, District Attorney Alex Hunter caved in to the pressure applied and summoned a grand jury. A grand jury is composed of ordinary citizens making a judgment call whether enough evidence is present to accuse a person of a crime.
A grand jury has subpoena power to demand evidence and witnesses but is separate from the judicial system.

This grand jury consisted of eight women and four men. They were presented all the evidence and, according to an anonymous grand juror in an ABC 20/20 interview, recommended charges to be filed against the Ramseys. Their decision was unsealed in 2013 under the Freedom of Information act. The grand jury decided to indict but fell short of stating the Ramseys killed JonBenét. The indictment counts IV(a) and VII are revealing about how the grand jury viewed the evidence.

The grand jury reached the conclusion that the Ramseys, "unlawfully, knowingly, recklessly and feloniously permit a child to be unreasonably placed in a situation which posed a threat of injury to the child's life or health, which resulted in the death of JonBenet Ramsey, a child under the age of sixteen".

And the Ramseys, "did unlawfully, knowingly and feloniously render assistance to a person, with intent to hinder, delay and prevent the discovery, detention, apprehension, prosecution, conviction and punishment of such person for the commission of a crime, knowing the person being assisted has committed and was suspected of the crime of Murder in the First Degree and Child Abuse Resulting in Death."

The wording of the grand jury shows official law language and implies they were assisted by a lawyer or law enforcement. And most interestingly, the Ramseys were not bundled in one statement, rather, both John and Patsy were individually accused. John and Patsy were individually represented by separate teams of lawyers.

The grand jury cited the Ramseys rendered assistance to, "a person knowing the person has committed murder". And these two words are loaded. The word "a" implies one person as opposed to a group. And "knowing" implies the Ramseys are aware of who the perpetrator is causing her death. It is unimaginable a parent, let alone both parents were motivated to elaborately plan to obscure, complicate, and confuse for a random intruder. The grand jury indictment tells us they believed the Ramseys covered for each other. They accused them separately because it was unclear who of the two parents killed JonBenét.

The grand jury perspective is in line with the answers John and Patsy on the Larry King Show: (Ramseys 2000):
King: "So you agree that whoever authored the ransom note probably killed the child?"
John Ramsey: "I agree."
Patsy Ramsey: "I would agree with that."

John committed to the answer and is consistent with a later reply, "I did not kill my daughter". John protects his wife through a fabricated intruder storyline and his denial Pats wrote the note.

Patsy did not commit to the author being the killer. She merely suggested she may agree which makes sense when you need to downplay because evidence shows she is the author of the note. The lack of commitment is in line with a future interview where she replied with, "I would knock his block [John] off".

Steve Thomas expected to find grieving parents the day he followed up with standard procedures. During fingerprinting, Patsy volunteered, "I did not kill my baby" and repeated, "I did not kill my baby" on request. A statement made is important enough for the speaker to be mentioned. She, likely on anxiety drugs, may have relived the event, was grieving, or tried to convince.

In my opinion, and that of other handwriting experts, Patsy wrote the ransom note. She was strongly motivated and convinced John to be part of an elaborate and bizarre plan. In the end, he decided to cooperate and that means there was something significant in it for him. Something so significant, it matched the horror of the child's death by the hand of the author of the ransom note. And that significant subject is unlikely two parents covering for Burke. They would agree and plan in unison. Patsy would not have to coerce John. That significant subject points most likely to the dictionary with its page dogeared pointing at incest.

District Attorney Alex Hunter was "the only game in town" and deeply embedded in the political atmosphere of Boulder, Colorado. Alex Hunter ordered the grand jury and to everyone's surprise, personally dismissed the grand jury's indictment citing there was not enough evidence. It is rare for a District Attorney to assemble a grand jury and not pursue their opinions. The real question is," Why?" And that brings us back to Alex Hunter's answer to Bill Hagmaier's question, "This is a political decision".

Exoneration

Mary Lacy, the District Attorney in 2008, wrote a carefully worded exoneration letter to John Ramsey citing, "new touch DNA tests and new evidence". The District Attorney exonerated the Ramseys in 2008 and wrote, "Significant new evidence has recently been discovered through the application of relatively new methods of DNA analysis."

Former lead Investigator for the District Attorney's office (1996), James Kolar wrote the new District Attorney in 2006 and stated, "If I am correct in my assessment, there may be a plausible explanation for the presence of the DNA in the underwear and it may have nothing to do with the death of JonBenét." (Kolar 2012)

Both statements are references to touch DNA found on JonBenét's clothing. We all leave traces of cells behind on anything we touch. We can use it for identification purposes by artificially developing minuscule DNA findings into strands of DNA. We leave DNA behind on a restaurant table where a murder took place. The touch DNA is developed, it belongs to you and that does not make you the murderer.

The touch DNA found on her clothing is not necessarily from the murderer. Studies have shown new packaged clothing and never worn also contains touch DNA. The source of the "new evidence" probably came from a factory worker handling the clothing item. My question is, "If touch DNA belonged to an intruder, why would it not be on other items related to JonBenét like the nylon cord, the paintbrush, the tape, etc.

District Attorney Lacy carefully worded the exoneration letter. "This new scientific evidence convinces us ....to state that we do not consider your immediate family...to be under any suspicion in the commission of this crime." She basically said, "we do not

consider you a suspect" which is not saying, "you had no involvement" or "did not do it".
"We are comfortable that the profile now in CODIS is the profile of the perpetrator of this murder". Again, the District Attorney said, "we are comfortable ...is the profile of the perpetrator". The use of "comfortable" is a qualifier. This is not a strong conviction and especially not when she also wrote: "probably handled by the perpetrator".

"We [District Attorney Office] intend in the future to treat you as the victims of this crime ...". Mary Lacy stated "intend to treat" which is not saying "we will treat you as the victims of this crime". Compare "I intend to go to the store" does not state I factually will. Mary Lacy, probably subconsciously, left the door open for future reference.

Oprah interviewed John in 2008 after he received the letter. His reaction to the exoneration was priceless. John interpreted the letter as, "a step in the right direction." He told everyone this is the first step and there is no finality to the case. There is a simple reason: He knows the intruder storyline is fabricated.

The touch DNA testing was performed by the Bode Technology Group at the District Attorney's request. They developed a profile and determined the profile consisted of more than one individual. The Bode Technologies lab report is dated March 24, 2008.

Bode Technologies Quote page 1 of 4:
"The DNA profile obtained from sample 2507-101-06A contains a mixture of at least two individuals including the victim and at least one male contributor. The profiles associated with the following individuals are excluded as possible contributors to the micro-DNA profile obtained from sample 2807-109-05A Burke Ramsey, Patricia Ramsey, John B. Ramsey, Melinda Ramsey, and John Andrew Ramsey".

Bode Technologies Quote page 2 of 4:
"It is known that the victim was wearing item 2807-101-05 the night of the crime therefore it is expected that the victim would be present in the samples associated with 2507-101-05. Assuming the victim, JonBenet Ramsey is a contributor, the remaining DNA contribution is provided in Table Two for samples 2507-101-05A and 2807-101-06B. Based on the results it's likely more than two people contributed to the mixtures observed in 2507-101-05A and 2507-101-058 therefore, the remaining DNA contribution should not be considered a single source profile".

Bode Technologies produced their report on March 24, 2008, or three months prior to the Mary Lacey exoneration letter dated July 9, 2008. Mary Lacy knew about the discrepancy and was a staunch supporter of the intruder theory.

Experts commented foreign DNA can come from a variety of innocent mechanisms. The 2008 exoneration letter included the line "… there is no innocent explanation for its incriminating presence." The sentence denied acknowledgment of her investigator Mr. Kolar in 2006. The word "incriminating" implies Ms. Lacy intended to use the DNA as hard evidence. The District Attorney was overriding the experts with her personal opinion or favored political will.

The exoneration letter made no sense then nor does it today. Multiple District Attorneys are on record denouncing the exoneration decision (Vaughan 2016). Former Adams County District Attorney Bob Grant said, "that just baffled my mind". Boulder District Attorney Stan Garret said, "I would not have done it because I do not think that is the role of the District Attorney". The former Governor Bill Owens said, "I was stunned. I…I…I was also appalled. There was no reason for her to do so". This begs the question: The then District Attorney has some explaining to do.

The final chapter

The JonBenét Ramsey saga continues to interest people since 1996 for a very good reason. The intruder theory is nonsense, does not match the evidence, and contradicts Patsy writing the ransom note. No parents decide as a team to protect a random murderer. The scene was staged and both parents kept each other in check. What they are hiding is something so significant, it outweighed years of anticipated scrutiny.

"Events that seem highly improbable in isolation become highly probable when large numbers of observations are considered".
– Nate Silver

Each data point is useless by itself in circumstantial evidence. Every storyline has a red thread protecting the best interest of a common source. The correlation between the data points reveals who benefits the most.

The JonBenét Ramsey data points are:
- The Ramseys arrive home around 10 pm.
  - Patsy is getting ready for an early flight the next day.
- Patsy Ramsey walked in on John Ramsey in a perceived compromising position.
  - The scenario is possible.
- Patsy Ramsey instantly enraged swings at John with the force to hit an adult.
  - John evades and turns JonBenét along with him.
  - Patsy accidentally hits JonBenét.
  - Patsy relived the event later by saying "I would knock his block off".
  - John downplayed the event as a "tragedy".
  - John downplayed the murderer to "this person".
  - Balance of Power scenario established.
    - i. Patsy murdered JonBenét.
    - ii. John stood to be accused of incest.

- Patsy and John are in shock and believe the child is dead.
  - They are in denial and do not know what to do.
  - The murder-incest scenario explains the alibi building theme.
  - Patsy or John looked up the definition of incest.
  - In their anxiety, they come up with a bizarre plan.
- Patsy is more motivated than John to cover it up.
  - Patsy is the author.
  - Patsy coerced John.
    i. "Listen carefully!"
    ii. "your situation"
    iii. "It is up to you now John!"
- Patsy writes the ransom note.
  - Patsy's handwriting is a match.
  - Patsy's linguistics match.
  - The author is an inept criminal.
  - The $118,000 matches a deferred payment.
  - Hints of alibi building to remove the body.
- Patsy and/or John stage the scene.
  - Duct tape had perfect lip prints.
  - JonBenét was unconscious and the tape was unnecessary.
  - The body was wrapped in a blanket and implies a caring attitude.
- The plan to remove the body failed.
  - Was it emotionally too difficult to put her body outside in the elements?
  - Did Rigor Mortis prevent her body to fit in a suitcase?
  - Were banks closed on December 26th, 1996?
- Patsy calls 911 at 5:52 am.
  - Patsy lacks urgency.
  - JonBenét is not a priority.
- Patsy opens the door fully dressed with hair and make-up intact at about 5:56 am.

- Patsy never went to bed.
- John lawyers up at 7:30 am.
  - The Ramseys were minimally cooperative.
- Patsy and John's behavior do not reflect two parents seeking to find their daughter.
  - No urgency.
  - John and Patsy did not console each other.
  - Nobody paid attention to the expected call.
- John was missing from around 11 am till noon.
  - John weighs his options and by 11 am he decided.
  - John went to the basement to apologize to JonBenét.
  - "He kissed and talked to her".
  - Detective Arndt noticed an increase in anxiety upon his return.
- John finds JonBenét at 1:05 pm.
  - John beelined to the basement.
  - John saw the body before switching the light on.
  - Fleet White said, "he knew where the body was".
  - Patsy stayed in the sunroom
  - Detective Arndt locked eyes with John and felt he knew what happened.
- John calls his pilot to get the plane ready at 1:40 pm.
  - Needed to leave the scene.
  - Abandoned JonBenét.
  - This suggests, "he is moving on" and is a phrase Burke used later.
- His two older children and fiancé arrived at 2:15 pm.
  - John tells them JonBenét is with Beth now.
  - John tells them they found JonBenét at 11 am.
  - 11 am matches the time he likely apologized.
- John and Patsy are minimally cooperative with law enforcement.
  - Team Ramsey shields them from the start.
- The coroner report comes out on December 27, 1996.

- – Asphyxia by strangulation.
- – Craniocerebral trauma.
- – Chronic inflammation vaginal mucosa.
- John and Patsy grant CNN a nationwide televised interview.
  - – An O.J. Simpson defense team strategic move to involve the public to taint the jury pool.
  - – He first thanks people for their support.
  - – Wants to know "why" to move on.
- John Ramsey defends Patsy robustly.
  - – Turns away from Anderson Cooper.
  - – Says, "Not even in a nanosecond".
  - – His voice pitches higher.
  - – Agrees the ransom note author is the killer.
- Patsy exaggerates her response to convince when pushed she was involved.
  - – "You are going down the wrong path here buddy!"
  - – "If John Ramsey was involved, I would knock his block off".
  - – "Read my lips. This was not done by a family member! Did not happen. Period. End of statement".
- Around the end of January 1997, Colorado Springs Police Department received an anonymous phone call claiming a pedophile ring killed JonBenét. The caller states it was an accident and a garrote was used.
  - – The garrote was not known by the general public.
  - – The pedophile ring was brought up for the first time.
  - – The Ramseys needed a reason for the chronic vaginal inflammation as reported by the coroner.
  - – John Ramsey pushed the pedophile scenario.
- The Ramseys were exonerated in 2008 from being suspects.
  - – John reacts with, "a step in the right direction".
  - – District Attorney Mary Lacy did not have a viable reason to exonerate.

The final chapter

It is very hard to convict someone on circumstantial evidence alone. Demonstrable evidence such as fingerprints, DNA, or a murder weapon needs to be presented. The only abstract and demonstrable evidence in the JonBenét Ramsey murder case is the ransom note. Patsy wrote the note beyond a reasonable doubt. The circumstantial evidence like the Ramsey's behaviors, what they said, and media manipulation point toward one common thread: The Ramseys. They know what happened. The correlation between the data points in behavior, statements, and context is essentially an admission of guilt in their own words and behavior.

What exactly happened that night remains an educated guess based on what we know. The scenario presented in this book is a viable option in gist but not necessarily correct in all the details. Perry Freeman, a former homicide detective, stated, "There is no known evidence that can challenge this theory" (Perry Freeman 2020). Something considerably dark happened which was important enough for the Ramseys to cover it up. The anticipated consequences outweighed years of scrutiny, the fear for prison, and their social standing.

Steve Thomas, the lead investigator, was right all along. In honor of Detective Thomas, I quote (Thomas 2000)[13]:
"But there are only two possible answers. One is that an intruder, known or unknown to the family, crept into the house, killed JonBenét in a botched kidnapping attempt while the family slept, then vanished, leaving behind what has been called the War and Peace of ransom notes, and then disappeared.

The other scenario is that the little girl was killed by a family member whom I believe to have been her panicked mother, Patsy Ramsey and that her father, John Ramsey, opted to protect his wife in the investigation that followed."

---

[13] Page 13

Clearly, I second the latter opinion as a Master Profiler through written communication. He continued with:

"The district attorney and his top prosecutor, two police chiefs, and a large number of cops, although so at odds on some points that they almost came to blows, all agreed on one thing—that probable cause existed to arrest Patsy Ramsey in connection with the death of her daughter. But due to a totally inept justice system in Boulder, no one was ever put in handcuffs, and the Ramseys were never really in serious jeopardy".

The District Attorney Office treated the Ramseys with kid's gloves. They gave them the same privileges as a charged suspect and exonerated them without a foundation to do so. In the end, JonBenét did not see justice served. It takes a village to raise a child and equally, it takes a village to cover up events. Many, if not most, abused children do not see justice served for various reasons. May this explanation of the ransom note and description of possible events put the case to rest and be the final chapter. The truth will eventually come out. Nobody lives in a vacuum and the event will have been shared. Someone knows and that someone will clear his or her conscience over time.

In my opinion, my theory is close to what happened that night in gist. Something unforeseen happened that night and both parents covered it up for. Exactly what happened that night in detail has not been determined as of yet.

With a horrible accident in mind and poor decisions made in an extremely stressful circumstance, the Ramseys have been punished enough with shame, guilt, and scrutiny. May JonBenét and Patsy rest in peace.

Summaries

Alleged intruder observations:
1. Wrote ransom note in the home.
    a. On Patsy's notepad.
    b. While parents sleeping upstairs.
    c. A two-and-a-half-page ransom note is too long.
2. Wrote the note after JonBenét's death
    a. Un harmed.
    b. Her to see 1997.
    c. She dies x 4.
3. Leaves body behind
    a. No kidnapper leaves their leverage for ransom behind.
4. Zero evidence an intruder was present
    a. No forced entry.
    b. The basement window is not the entry point.
5. The intruder did not write from experiential memory
    a. Hence a[sic] earlier ~~delivery~~ pick-up.
    b. We do \not/ like.
    c. From a group perspective to a personal perspective back to a group perspective.
    d. Monitor/ scrutiny do not match the two if statements.
6. Hints of alibi building
    a. We just got up.
    b. Bring adequate attaché.
    c. Fear exaggeration: she dies x 4.
7. Intruder knows John intimately
    a. From Mr. Ramsey to John.
    b. From your account.
    c. Southern common sense.
    d. $118,000.
8. The note has three parts
    a. Demands – Hedges - Pleads
    b. No kidnapper relinquishes control.

Patsy observations:
1. Deceptive 911 call.
    a. Did not prioritize JonBenét.
    b. Did not create authentic urgency.
    c. Hints of alibi building.
2. The ransom note author matches Patsy in:
    a. Handwriting.
    b. Emotional impact.
    c. Personality.
    d. Word selection.
    e. Inept criminal tendencies.
    f. Knows John intimately.
    g. Alibi building.
3. Behavior
    a. Did not pay attention to the expected phone call.
    b. Patsy did not console John.
    c. Eyes Officer French through her fingers after he came back from the basement.
    d. Did not come off her seat when JonBenét was brought upstairs.

There are no coincidences. Don Foster: "Individuals are prisoners of their own language". Patsy matches the author emotionally, behaviorally, in her handwriting, and word selection. The chances an intruder matches someone in the home with this many similarities is zero-point-nihil.

John observations:
1. Did not pay attention to the expected phone call.
2. Did not console Patsy.
3. No urgency in the CNN interview.
   a. Prioritized thanking people.
4. Was missing from 11 am till noon.
   a. Increased anxiety upon return from being missing.
5. Finds body at 1 pm.
   a. Beelined to the basement.
   b. Saw the body before the light was switched on.
6. Downplaying the event.
   a. From murder to tragedy.
   b. Needs to know "why" instead of "what".
   c. There is no answer.
   d. My mission for the rest of my life.
7. Assists in writing the ransom note.
   a. Monitor, execute, electronic, device, percentages.
8. Exaggerates protection of Patsy
   a. Not even in a nano-second.
   b. Suddenly looks away from Anderson Cooper.

Burke observations:
1. Is believed to have asked "what did you find?" on the 911 call.
2. Boulder Police Department never saw him as a suspect.
3. A child psychologist interpreted Burke's interview as typical for a child who is not allowed to share information.
4. Burke appears to repeat what adults say to each other
   a. "getting on with my life."
5. Strong answers on Dr. Phil show
   a. I know that is not what happened.
   b. I know I did not do it.

Deception tactics observed

A summary of the recognized deception methods used by the Ramseys.

1. Baseline: habit.
    a. John painfully wailing over the death of Beth while being stoic and cordial about JonBenét.
    b. John suddenly looking away in the Anderson Cooper interview when asked about Patsy's involvement.
    c. Patsy, the social butterfly, makes herself needed yet stayed in the sunroom when JonBenét's body was brought upstairs.
2. Word selection: a change in a word is a change in reality.
    a. Patsy 911 call:
        i. A kidnapping.
        ii. A note.
        iii. Gone.
    b. John CNN interview:
        i. Why.
        ii. For the rest of my life.
3. Downplaying: euphemisms.
    a. John: Murder to tragedy
    b. John: Murderer to this person
4. Exaggeration: a tactic to convince.
    a. Patsy: "you're going down the wrong path, buddy".
    b. Patsy: "read my lips! This was not done by a family member".
    c. Patsy: "Did not happen. Period. End of story".
    d. Ransom note: "she dies" (x 4)
    e. John: "not even in a nano-second"
5. Gaslighting: destabilizing others.
    a. John: "incest is just ridiculous" [not verbatim] is a personal attack on the intelligence of the claimant.

    b. John: "It was a pedophile intruder who had a key and stayed in the house during the day" is making others question their reality and sanity.

6. Freudian slips: hidden experiences.
    a. Patsy said JonBenét was "gone" in the 911 call. The word "gone" may mean "dead" or "not to be found".
    b. John found JonBenét at 1 pm and told the arriving family members at 11 am

7. Deflection: redirection.
    a. The rambling ransom note with unusual instructions distracts the reader.
    b. The anonymous pedophile ring calls the Colorado Springs Police Department.

8. Evasion: truth without critical details.
    a. Interviewer: "do you agree the author of the ransom note is the killer?" John: "I agree" and omits he knows who did.

9. Changes in recollection
    a. Patsy changed her story from seeing the ransom note first then checking the bedroom and later reversed the sequence.
    b. John changed his story from finding JonBenét's body to switching the light on to not recalling he switched the light on.
    c. John changed his story from screaming when he saw JonBenét's body to he kissed and talked to her.
    d. John changed his story from reading to both children before going to bed to not having read to them.

Addendums

Ransom Note page 1

1 Mr. Ramsey,
2   Listen carefully! We are a
3 group of individuals that represent
4 a small foreign faction. We do
5 respect your bussiness but not the
6 country that it serves. At this
7 time we have your daughter in our
8 posession. She is safe and unharmed
9 and if you want her to see 1997,
10 you must follow our instructions to
11 the letter.
12   You will withdraw $118,000.00
13 from your account. $100,000 will be
14 in $100 bills and the remaining
15 $18,000 in $20 bills. Make sure
16 that you bring an adequate size
17 attache to the bank. When you
18 get home you will put the money
19 in a brown paper bag. I will
20 call you between 8 and 10 am
21 tomorrow to instruct you on delivery.
22 The delivery will be exhausting so
23 I advise you to be rested. If
24 we monitor you getting the money
25 eatly, we might call you early to
26 arrange an earlier delivery of the -

Ransom Note page 2

27 money and hence a earlier
28 ~~delivery~~ pick-up of your daughter.
29 Any deviation of my instructions
30 will result in the immediate
31 execution of your daughter. You
32 will also be denied her remains
33 for proper burial. The two
34 gentlemen watching over your daughter
35 do particularly like you so I
36 advise you not to provoke them.
37 Speaking to anyone about your
38 situation, such as Police, F.B.I., etc.,
39 will result in your daughter being
40 beheaded. If we catch you talking
41 to a stray dog, she dies. If you
42 alert bank authorities, she dies.
43 If the money is in any way
44 marked or tampered with, she
45 dies. You will be scanned for
46 electronic devices and if any are
47 found, she dies. You can try to
48 deceive us but be warned that
49 we are familiar with law enforcement
50 countermeasures and tactics. You
51 stand a 99% chance of killing
52 your daughter if you try to out
53 smart us. Follow our instructions

Ransom Note page 3

54 and you stand a 100% chance
55 of getting her back. You and
56 your family are under constant
57 scutiny as well as the authorities.
58 Don't try to grow a brain
59 John. You are not the only
60 fat cat around so don't think
61 that killing will be difficult
62 Don't underestimate us John.
63 Use that good southern common
64 sense of yours. It is up to
65 you now John!

66
67

Victory!

S.B.T.C

Coroner report page 1

Post Office Box 471 • Boulder, Colorado 80306

Office of the Boulder County Coroner
1777 6th Street • Boulder County Justice Center • Boulder, Colorado 80302 • (303) 441-3535

AUTOPSY REPORT

NAME:	RAMSEY, JONBENET		AUTOPSY NO:	96A-155
DOB:	08/06/90		DEATH D/T:	12/26/96 @ 1323
AGE:	6Y		AUTOPSY D/T:	12/27/96 @ 0815
SEX:	F		ID NO:	137712
PATH MD:	MEYER		COR/MEDREC#:	1714-96-A
TYPE:	COR			

FINAL DIAGNOSIS:

    I.   Ligature strangulation
        A. Circumferential ligature with associated ligature
            furrow of neck
        B. Abrasions and petechial hemorrhages, neck
        C. Petechial hemorrhages, conjunctival surfaces of eyes
            and skin of face
   II. Craniocerebral injuries
        A. Scalp contusion
        B. Linear, comminuted fracture of right side of skull
        C. Linear pattern of contusions of right cerebral
            hemisphere
        D. Subarachnoid and subdural hemorrhage
        E. Small contusions, tips of temporal lobes
 III. Abrasion of right cheek
  IV. Abrasion/contusion, posterior right shoulder
   V. Abrasions of left lower back and posterior left lower
        leg
  VI. Abrasion and vascular congestion of vaginal mucosa
 VII. Ligature of right wrist

Toxicologic Studies

blood ethanol - none detected
blood drug screen - no drugs detected

CLINICOPATHOLOGIC CORRELATION: Cause of death of this six year old
female is asphyxia by strangulation associated with craniocerebral
trauma.

John E. Meyer, M.D.
John E. Meyer, M.D.
Pathologist

jn/12/27/96

Mary Lacy exoneration letter page 1

DISTRICT ATTORNEY S OFFICE
TWENTIETH JUDICIAL DISTRICT

MARY T LACY, DISTRICT ATTORNEY

July 9, 2008

Mr. John Ramsey

Dear Mr. Ramsey,

As you are aware, since December 2002, the Boulder District Attorney's Office has been the agency responsible for the investigation of the homicide of your daughter, JonBenet. I understand that the fact that we have not been able to identify the person who killed her is a great disappointment that is a continuing hardship for you and your family.

However, significant new evidence has recently been discovered through the application of relatively new methods of DNA analysis. This new scientific evidence convinces us that it is appropriate, given the circumstances of this case, to state that we do not consider your immediate family, including you, your wife, Patsy, and your son, Burke, to be under any suspicion in the commission of this crime. I wish we could have done so before Mrs. Ramsey died.

We became aware last summer that some private laboratories were conducting a new methodology described as "touch DNA." One method of sampling for touch DNA is the "scraping method." This is a process in which forensic scientists scrape places where there are no stains or other signs of the possible presence of DNA to recover for analysis any genetic material that might nonetheless be present. We contracted with the Bode Technology Group, a highly reputable laboratory recommended to us by several law enforcement agencies, to use the scraping method for touch DNA on the long johns that JonBenet wore and that were probably handled by the perpetrator during the course of this crime.

The Bode Technology laboratory was able to develop a profile from DNA recovered from the two sides of the long johns. The previously identified profile from the crotch

Boulder Office: Justice Center • 1777 6ᵗʰ Street • Boulder, Colorado 80302 • (303) 441-3700 • Fax: (303) 441-4703
Longmont Office: 1035 Kimbark • Longmont, Colorado 80501 • (303) 441-3700 • Fax: (303) 682-6711
TDD/V (303) 441-4774 • Internet: http:/www.co.boulder.co.us/da • E-mail: boulder.da@co.boulder.co.us

160

Mary Lacy exoneration letter page 2

of the underwear worn by JonBenet at the time of the murder matched the DNA recovered from the long johns at Bode.

Unexplained DNA on the victim of a crime is powerful evidence. The match of male DNA on two separate items of clothing worn by the victim at the time of the murder makes it clear to us that an unknown male handled these items. Despite substantial efforts over the years to identify the source of this DNA, there is no innocent explanation for its incriminating presence at three sites on these two different items of clothing that JonBenet was wearing at the time of her murder.

Solving this crime remains our goal, and its ultimate resolution will depend on more than just matching DNA. However, given the history of the publicity surrounding this case, I believe it is important and appropriate to provide you with our opinion that your family was not responsible for this crime. Based on the DNA results and our serious consideration of all the other evidence, we are comfortable that the profile now in CODIS is the profile of the perpetrator of this murder.

To the extent that we may have contributed in any way to the public perception that you might have been involved in this crime, I am deeply sorry. No innocent person should have to endure such an extensive trial in the court of public opinion, especially when public officials have not had sufficient evidence to initiate a trial in a court of law. I have the greatest respect for the way you and your family have handled this adversity.

I am aware that there will be those who will choose to continue to differ with our conclusion. But DNA is very often the most reliable forensic evidence we can hope to find and we rely on it often to bring to justice those who have committed crimes. I am very comfortable that our conclusion that this evidence has vindicated your family is based firmly on all of the evidence, including the reliable forensic DNA evidence that has been developed as a result of advances in that scientific field during this investigation.

2

Mary Lacy exoneration letter page 3

We intend in the future to treat you as the victims of this crime, with the sympathy due you because of the horrific loss you suffered. Otherwise, we will continue to refrain from publicly discussing the evidence in this case.

We hope that we will one day obtain a DNA match from the CODIS data bank that will lead to further evidence and to the solution of this crime. With recent legislative changes throughout the country, the number of profiles available for comparison in the CODIS data bank is growing steadily. Law enforcement agencies are receiving increasing numbers of cold hits on DNA profiles that have been in the system for many years. We hope that one day soon we will get a match to this perpetrator. We will, of course, contact you immediately. Perhaps only then will we begin to understand the psychopathy or motivation for this brutal and senseless crime.

Respectfully,

Mary T. Lacy
District Attorney
Twentieth Judicial District
Boulder, Colorado

Bode technologies page 1

Bode Technology.

10430 Furnace Road, Suite 107
Lorton, VA 22079
Phone: 703-646-9740

Forensic Case Report
March 24, 2008

To:
Andy Horita
Boulder District Attorney's Office   **BODE Case #:** 2S07-101
1777 6ᵗʰ Street   **Agency Case #:** 96DA21871
Boulder, CO 80302

List of Evidence Received on December 3, 2007 for possible DNA analysis:

BODE Sample #	Agency Description
2S07-101-01	Labeled as "Ligature from neck. BPD# 022TET, CBI# 006"
2S07-101-02	Labeled as "Broken paintbrush handle (attached to #1 above)"
2S07-101-03	Labeled as "Ligature from wrist. BPD # 018TET, CBI # 166"
2S07-101-04	Labeled as "Wednesday" panties. BPD #021TET, CBI# 7"
2S07-101-05	Labeled as "White long underwear bottoms. BPD020TET, CBI # 5"
2S07-101-05A	exterior top right half of long johns
2S07-101-05B	exterior top left half of long johns
2S07-101-05C	interior top right half of long johns
2S07-101-05D	interior top left half of long johns

List of Evidence Received on January 23, 2008 for possible DNA analysis:

BODE Sample #	Agency Description
2S07-101-06	Labeled as "Cutting from crotch of underwear. BPD# 110KKY"
2S07-101-06A	cutting from top layer
2S07-101-06B	cutting from top layer opposite of -06A
2S07-101-06C	cutting from bottom layer same edge as -06A

Table One contains Profiler Plus and Cofiler data submitted on March 12, 2008 for the following samples:

BPD #	CBI	Description
001BP	148	Blood standard JonBenet-Victim
5RTG	36B-2	Blood Standards Burke Ramsey-Brother
4RTG/009TET	35B-2	Blood Standards Patricia Ramsey-Mother
3RTG/008TET	34B-2	Blood Standards John B. Ramsey-Father
2RTG/72TET	33B-2	Blood Standard Melinda Ramsey- ½ Sister (Common Father)
1RTG	32B-2	Blood Standards John Andrew Ramsey- ½ Brother (Common Father)

DNA PROCESSING, RESULTS, and CONCLUSIONS:

The evidence items were processed for DNA typing by analysis of the 13 CODIS Short Tandem Repeat loci, the D2S1338 locus, the D19S433 locus, and the gender determining locus Amelogenin using the AmpFLSTR® Identifiler® kit. Appropriate positive and negative controls were used concurrently throughout the analysis. The DNA profiles reported in this case were determined by procedures that have been validated according to standards established by the Scientific Working Group on DNA Analysis Methods (SWGDAM) and adopted as Federal Standards.

1. The DNA profile obtained from sample 2S07-101-05A contains a mixture of at least two individuals including the victim and at least one male contributor. The profiles associated with the following individuals are excluded as possible contributors to the mixture DNA profile obtained from sample 2S07-101-05A: Burke Ramsey, Patricia Ramsey, John B. Ramsey, Melinda Ramsey, and John Andrew Ramsey.

Page 1 of 4

135

Body Technologies page 2

BODE Case #: 2S07-101
Agency Case #: 96DA21871

Date: March 24, 2008

DNA PROCESSING, RESULTS, and CONCLUSIONS (cont.):

2. The partial DNA profile obtained from sample 2S07-101-05B contains a mixture of at least two individuals including the victim and at least one male contributor. The profiles associated with the following individuals are excluded as possible contributors to the mixture DNA profile obtained from sample 2S07-101-05B: John B. Ramsey, Melinda Ramsey, and John Andrew Ramsey. The profiles associated with Burke Ramsey and Patricia Ramsey cannot be included or excluded from the mixture DNA profile obtained from 2S07-101-05B.

3. The partial DNA profile obtained from sample 2S07-101-05C contains a mixture of at least two individuals including a major component victim profile and at least one additional minor contributor. The minor contributor is low level, contains allelic drop-out, and therefore is not suitable for comparison.

4. The DNA profile obtained from sample 2S07-101-05D contains a mixture of at least three individuals including the victim and at least one male contributor. Due to the complexity of this mixture it was deemed unsuitable for any further comparison purposes.

5. Samples 2S07-101-05A, -05B, and -05C were combined and processed as -05X. The partial DNA profile obtained from sample 2S07-101-05X is consistent with the victim.

See **Table Two** for summary of alleles reported for these samples.

NOTES:

1. It is known that the victim was wearing item 2S07-101-05 the night of the crime; therefore it is expected that the victim would be present in the samples associated with 2S07-101-05. Assuming the victim, JonBenet Ramsey is a contributor, the remaining DNA contribution is provided in Table Two for samples 2S07-101-05A and 2S07-101-05B. Based on the results it is likely more than two people contributed to the mixtures observed in 2S07-101-05A and 2S07-101-05B therefore, the remaining DNA contribution should not be considered a single source profile.

2. Samples 2S07-101-01, -02, -03, and -04 were not processed at this time.

3. The DNA extracts and submitted evidence will be returned to Andy Horita at the Boulder District Attorney's Office.

Report submitted by:

Amy Jeanguenat, MFS
DNA Analyst II

Page 2 of 4

References

department, IGAS instruction. 1994. *Fears and defenses.*

Diego, CNN Carmen San. 2019. *The murder of JonBenét.* July 19. https://www.youtube.com/watch?v=WLKsEEcINyo&t=188s.

Dines, Jess E. 1998. *Document Examiner textbook.* Pantex International.

Douglas, John, and Olshaker, Mark. 1999. *The anatomy of motive.*

Elfers, Marcel. 2016. *One Reason.*

—. 2018. *School shooter.* CreateSpace; an Amazon company.

Foster, Don. 2000. *Author unknown.*

Hodges, Andrew G, M.D. 1998. *A mother gone bade.*

Iannetta, Kimon S., and Craine, James F, Ph.D. 2008. *Danger between the lines.*

investigation., JonBenét. Anatomy of an. 2000. https://www.youtube.com/watch?v=CXMNPU75lbw.

Jury, Grand. n.d. *Colorado Judicial Branch.* https://www.courts.state.co.us/Media/Opinion_Docs/JRams ey%20Grand%20Jury.pdf.

Kimble, Lindsay. 2016. October 4. https://people.com/celebrity/911-operator-in-jonbenet-ramsey-case-says-call-seemed-reheased/.

Kolar, A. James. 2012. *Foreign Faction.*

McClish, Mark. 2012. *I know you are lying.*

McNichol, Andrea and Nelson, Jeffrey. 1991. *Handwriting Analysis; Putting it to work for you.*

Meyer, John E. n.d. *autopsyfiles.org.* http://www.autopsyfiles.org/reports/Other/ramsey,%20jonbenet_autopsy.pdf.

NAPCAN. n.d. https://www.napcan.org.au/.

Neuman, Scott. 2013. *NPR news.* October 25. https://www.npr.org/sections/thetwo-way/2013/10/25/240749945/unsealed-documents-shine-light-on-jonbenet-murder-case.

Pereda, Guilera, Forns and Gomez-Benito. 2009. https://pubmed.ncbi.nlm.nih.gov/19371992/.

Perry Freeman, Former Colorado Springs Police Department Homicide Detective. 2020. July 29. https://www.youtube.com/watch?v=AwJn4nRvQAQ.

Ramsey, John, interview by Anderson Cooper. 2012. (March 14).

Ramsey, John, and Patsy. 2001. *The death of innocence.*

Ramseys, interview by Larry King. 2000. *The Larry King Show* (May 31).

Riso, Don and Hudson, Russ. n.d. *The Enneagram Institute.* https://www.enneagraminstitute.com/type-2.

Riso, Don Richard, and Hudson, Russ. 1996. *Personality Types; Using the Enneagram for Self-Discovery (1996).*

Schiller, Lawrence. 1999. *Perfect Murder, Perfect Town.*

n.d. *soiled long johns JonBenét.* https://external-preview.redd.it/71HJEbDzAMMqJzqD66QSWLbLLl5gkD5h meUvFztKS24.jpg?s=336313807d0fb5fce7f1286c1b659e2 15481190f.

Stout, Martha. 2006. *the sociopath next door.*

Thomas, Steve. 2000. *JonBenét, inside the Ramsey murder investigation.* St. Martin's Press.

Vaughan, Kevin. 2016. *DNA in Doubt, the JonBenet Ramsey case.* December 27. https://www.youtube.com/watch?v=GT7YEPVAPiQ.

2016. *We have your daughter.* November. http://www.wehaveyourdaughter.net/dna-evidence/2017/3/2/bode-technology-written-analysis-on-dna-in-the-jonbent-ramsey-case.

Wecht, Cyril H., and Bosworth, Charles. 1998. *Who killed JonBenét Ramsey?*

n.d. *Wikipedia.* https://en.wikipedia.org/wiki/Locard%27s_exchange_princi ple.

Wong, Cina. 2016. *Investigation Discovery.* September 13. https://www.youtube.com/watch?v=1JM7bO7beNA.

n.d. *YouTube.* https://www.youtube.com/watch?v=hGsUQF0kp_w.

Bibliography

Douglas, John, and Olshaker, Mark: *The anatomy of motive* (1999)

Elfers, Marcel D.: *JonBenét. The Graphologist, the journal of the British Institute of Graphologists.* (Fall 2015, vol. 33, no. 3.)

Elfers, Marcel D.: *One Reason; an overview of likeability.* (2017)

Foster, Don W.: *Author unknown.* (2000)

Iannetta, Kimon S., and Craine, James F, Ph.D.: *Danger between the lines, a reference manual for the profiling of violent behavior.* (2008)

IGAS instruction department: *Fears and defenses* (1994)

Kolar, James A.: *Foreign Faction, who really kidnapped JonBénet* (2012)

McClish, Mark: *I know you are lying* (2012)

McNichol, Andrea, and Nelson, Jeffrey A.: *Handwriting analysis, putting it to work for you* (1991,1994)

Palmer, Helen: *The Enneagram, understanding yourself and the others in your life.* (1991)

Ramsey, John, and Patsy: *The death of innocence* (2001)

Riso, Don Richard, and Hudson, Russ: *Personality Types: Using the Enneagram for Self-Discovery* (1996)

Riso, Don Richard, and Hudson, Russ: *The wisdom of the Enneagram, the complete guide to psychological and spiritual growth for the nine personality types* (1999)

Smith, Laurence L: *"The last Christmas of JonBenét Ramsey"* *(updated through 2015)*

Stout, Martha: *"the sociopath next door"* (2006)

Schiller, Lawrence: *Perfect Town, Perfect Murder* (1999)

Seifer, Mark, Ph.D.: *The Definitive Book of handwriting analysis* (2009)

Thomas, Steve, and Davis, Donald A.: *JonBénet, inside the murder investigation* (2000)

Wecht, Cyril, M.D.: *Who killed JonBenét Ramsey?* (1998)

Made in United States
Troutdale, OR
12/29/2024